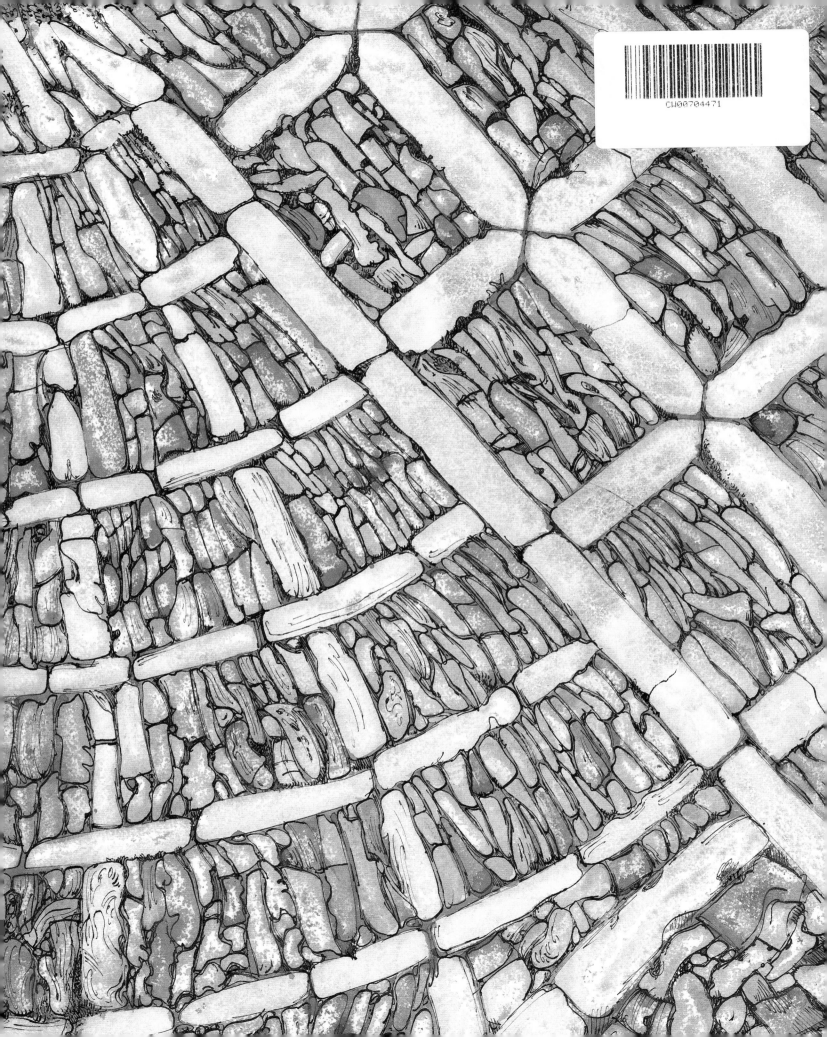

David Gentleman's Italy

Hadrian's Villa, Tivoli

David Gentleman's Italy

Hodder & Stoughton

Neptune's Fountain, Bologna

© 1997 by David Gentleman

First published in 1997
by Hodder and Stoughton
A division of Hodder Headline PLC

The right of David Gentleman to be identified as the author of
this work has been asserted by him in accordance with the
Copyright, Designs and Patents Act 1988.

10 9 8 7 6 5 4 3 2 1

A catalogue record for this book
is available from the British Library

ISBN 0 340 64912 7

Photoset by Rowland Phototypesetting Ltd,
Bury St Edmunds, Suffolk

Printed and bound in Great Britain by
Butler & Tanner Ltd, Frome and London

Hodder and Stoughton Ltd
A division of Hodder Headline PLC
338 Euston Road
London NW1 3BH

Contents

Introduction

Italy is a beautiful country, energetic, inventive and civilised, stimulating to visit and lovely to draw. It has at different periods enjoyed great power and creativity – relics of both abound – and is lucky in having lost the one but kept the other. It seldom reminds one of anyplace else: wherever you turn, things look Italian. Italy's problems are universal ones but its triumphs and beauties are unique.

The country is not vast in area, being slim and peninsular rather than broad and continental like say France, but its narrow leg-shaped form extends a long way, from the cool Alps to the almost African landscapes of Sicily – alpine plants and shattered firs in the north, cacti and prickly pears in the south. It has its vast fat prosperous plains like the Po Valley, but most Italian landscapes include the pale mountainous distances that look so lovely in early Italian paintings. There are rushing rivers and beautiful lakes. The mountains are big and craggy and made of marble; rounded hills and lush plains alike are intensively but picturesquely cultivated, patterned by lines of vines and dotted with blue-grey olives. The fields are hidden beneath jungles of maize, or ablaze with yellow sunflowers, or glowing with ripening wheat; at harvest time cylindrical bales of straw lie strewn on the golden stubble like the tumbled Doric columns of Selinunte. The woods are dark and dense, full of hoopoes and owls and wild boar; the summer skies are alive with swifts and buzzards, the streams with croaking frogs, the rocky southern uplands with green lizards and black snakes. The peninsula is surrounded by the tideless Mediterranean which, though now and then looking a bit polluted, is usually clear and full of many sizes of fish.

The much-noted Italian light, while naturally intense and glaring at midsummer, is just as variable as elsewhere. The Italian climate allows sociable activities like eating and drinking and meeting one another to go on out of doors for most of the year; from February to November the human scene unrolls in full view, not hidden away indoors. All these things are interesting to draw.

A typical Italian landscape will usually include gentle hills stretching away to hazy mountains. In the middle distance are olive groves and patches or strips of woodland, and wheat fields with lines of vines and isolated mulberry trees standing in the crop, or sunflowers or maize, or smaller crops like cabbage; in the foreground are grass and poppies, birds and butterflies. Brightly coloured new tractors and combines crawl over the fields; there are people on scooters or mopeds and heavy lorries full of grain or fertiliser on the narrow white stone-chip roads that wind between them; further away, a main road carries a steadier flow of traffic and one can glimpse cars and lorries glinting in the sun on a distant motorway. Dotted about are farmhouses, the older ones often abandoned, the newer standing amid strongly built concrete barns and sheds. On the distant hilltops one can see walled villages tightly hemmed in round a church tower or dome, with newer-looking houses scattered more randomly in the fields beyond the village confines. The ploughing bullock teams that I remember from my earliest visits have long disappeared, but occasionally one may still see a tall round haystack formed round an upright pole and getting slenderer and more angular as the hay is sliced sharply away for fodder.

Via dei Servi, Florence

But it isn't the wild untouched landscapes – less built-up the farther south one goes – or even the painstakingly and lovingly cultivated hillsides, that attract me particularly to Italy. Rather it's the presence in these beautiful landscapes of brick and stone – of the farms, castles, villages, towns and cities that are a magical part of the Italian scene, and which I've mainly drawn. They belong to and seem to grow out of the landscape, crowning an eminence, spreading and enhancing a hollow, or gradually replacing a rural with an urban scene. In Italy, landscape and settlement form a partnership. From the fields one sees villages and towns, and in the towns and cities one is still aware of the surrounding country: Etna from Taormina, the mountains north of Turin or inland from Lucca, the big hills rising behind Genoa or Palermo or encircling Florence or Siena, the tree-dotted and hummocky hillocks round Urbino or Todi, the arid bleakness round Volterra. Only in the biggest or flattest places – Rome, Milan, Venice – can one forget the surrounding countryside entirely.

Venice

Drawing a building makes you look hard at it: first making sure it's the subject you really want to spend time on, and then – in order to understand what it really looks like and how it works – studying its structure, proportions, details, quirks. Drawing makes you see buildings not in isolation but as they relate to each other and their setting – standing perhaps on a slight slope, or at the key point where a street almost imperceptibly changes direction; facing other buildings across a broad space, or one so narrow that you can see only a thin sliver of sky; standing in deep shadow or lit by the strong Italian sun; the windows wide open or ajar behind half-closed shutters, festooned with flowers or hidden behind drying washing. You'd probably take all these things in sooner or later without paying them much attention, but drawing hastens and concentrates the process and encourages your eye to move on from the basic practicalities – bar, restaurant, cashpoint – to these other more interesting things.

Throughout the day, the Italian street is a fascinating place to draw in. There are certain basic elements: houses, shops, cafés, archways, cool and shady arcades, a church, a palace now used by a bank, probably a piazza to one side. There are the optional extras: fountains, flights of steps, statues of people and horses, obelisks, Roman remains, trees, signs, metro entrances and bus stops, newsagents' kiosks that open and shut like great umbrellas; all of them fairly permanent. There are also other more temporary items: market stalls, African hawkers' neat pavement layouts of handbags and photo posters and trinkets. Then there are various wheeled things: street-cleaners on tricycles, mechanised rubbish carts, big rubbish bins on castors, ice-cream and cold-drink trolleys, pony and donkey carts for children to ride in, jingling horse-drawn landaus for grown-ups, and parked bikes and scooters for teenagers to perch, chat and show themselves off on. And finally there are the foot-soldiers: beggars, musicians, flower sellers, various kinds of policemen, monks and nuns, parking women, balloon-sellers, pickpockets, spectacularly uniformed cadets, children, cats and pigeons. All of these too are good to watch and to draw.

Anyone who draws on the streets in Italy will meet plenty of people. Those I talked to were friendly, curious, intelligent and cultivated, generous and outgoing, and patient with my bad Italian. Those I drew looked vivacious and energetic, with the easy unselfconsciousness and the emphatic stance and gesture that one tends to think of as theatrical or operatic. Drawing the Italians as they shopped or talked or telephoned or drank coffee made me feel that ordinary daily living is itself a kind of art, expressive and beautiful.

There are different kinds of beauty. Hills and cultivated fields looks beautiful by accident – no one has designed them or given their appearance much thought. Palaces, fruit stalls, clothes, fashion models on the other hand all look good by *trying* – it's their job to. And somewhere between accident and design there is a third kind of beauty, that of houses and streets and squares, places that have come to look well because of circumstances, not altogether arranged on purpose but valued and cherished all the same because over many years things as well as people have conspired to make them as they are. This is not just for a cultivated élite. This kind of beauty is one that every Italian recognises and enjoys; for in Italy, beauty – the way things look – counts.

Italy and Britain have certain affinities and similarities. Both once had great empires, the Roman one lasting for many centuries. In Rome, the remnants of this power, wealth, importance and self-confidence – columns, temples, theatres, vast baths, the Colosseum, the Pantheon, Trajan's column, the Pyramid – are not only picturesque but impressive and disquieting. Besides making good subjects, they make you think. To a Londoner, many of the Roman antiquities also look oddly familiar, reminding one of the British Museum portico or the Duke of York's column or of the façade of a London club. Whenever anything in Italy looks familiar to English eyes, however, it's because we've copied it – never the other way round. Yet even this apparently rather lowly process of imitation has been a vital element in British architectural development.

Rome

Not only architects – Inigo Jones, Kent, Burlington – and their patrons on the Grand Tour, but English writers and artists have been drawn to Italy, been inspired or turned on there, and become part of it. In the Piazza di Spagna one thinks of Keats and Shelley, on the Capitol and in the Baths of Caracalla of Gibbon, in Santa Croce in Florence of E. M. Forster, in Venice of Ruskin – I chanced to stay for a day or two in the pretty canalside hotel where he once lived. Italy's landscapes and archaeological remains have long provided architects with inspiration, and artists with subject-matter and a livelihood; and their images have proved very durable. When one tries to call to mind a Roman or Venetian scene one sees it through the eyes of Piranesi or Canaletto. Poussin and Claude and Corot lived in Italy or built their fame on their Italian experience; and many English painters went to work there too – artists as diverse as Cozens, Wilson, Turner, Lear, and Sickert. Such artists created their own personal visions of Italy, versions that overlaid the realities of a country that relatively few of their contemporaries could ever hope to see. Now almost anyone who really wants to can go there and see for himself; one of the pleasures of going there now is recognising and checking up on the scenes these artists painted. But the overall reality one discovers is both richer and more unsettling than the familiar and comforting visions of Guardi and Longhi and Turner. Reconciling these opposites – vision and reality, past and present – offers both pleasures and surprises.

In Italy, the past is always close at hand. Often it takes spectacular form: Greek temples, Roman forums, Moorish cathedrals, Byzantine basilicas, medieval castles and towers and walled cities, Renaissance domes, nineteenth-century Gallerias, splendid ruins from all periods. But the past survives just as vividly in humbler and more ordinary things: in walls, arches, pavements, bits of carved stone; in small intimate details like the well-made iron rings for tethering horses that have been set into palace walls, even in the nails patterning an ancient door much as the olive trees pattern the beautiful Italian hillsides.

One needn't be much of a student of architecture or even of history to sense the range and richness of Italy's architectural evolution. Its very wealth may seem confusing at first, but as you draw or look carefully at buildings you begin to see their development not as a confused welter of styles chosen at random but each as part of an inevitable evolution. The process has been carried out over millennia: successive generations of builders doing what they could with the available materials and techniques, extending them if need be, and applying these skills to a wide variety of structures from the minimal and simple to the immense and monumental. Naturally, only a few of the very simplest buildings remain – cave dwellings at Matera, beehive *trulli* on the nearby plains. Though puzzling at first, this steady development – from these brutish caves, through Rome and the Renaissance to today's high-rises and motorways – is not really very hard to grasp; the evolution gradually comes to seem inevitable and logical. What is uniquely Italian about this progress is its continuity and timespan. Whereas Greek architecture rather petered out after Paestum and the Parthenon, the Italians have stuck at it, one breakthrough and climax after another, right up to the present day: through the daringly inventive engineering of the nineteenth century, practical yet flamboyant, and the eventual swing back to the austere concrete, glass and steel of today.

In Britain, our history is in layers, the oldest below, the newest on top; the ancient past is something that has to be dug up. But in Italy old and new often still exist side by side: a classical Temple of Minerva at Assisi next to a medieval church, a Greek temple in Siracusa boxed in within a baroque cathedral, a splendid Roman colonnade in the heart of Milan separated from a medieval basilica by a nineteenth-century tramway. In Italy we can follow the development of architecture from the simple structures and forms, the straight lines, planes, arcs and circles of Greece and Rome and Byzantium, to the curving, swirling and billowing façades of the baroque, in Rome and Naples and the south. And we can savour the contrast between the geometric,

Milan

almost undecorated façades of the north and the riotous southern ornament of Apulia and Sicily: for even within Italy herself we can see the contrast of northern values and attitudes – sceptical, puritanical, sober – with southern sensuality, voluptuousness, faith: warm, credulous and silly.

European architecture began with the Greeks, but the best-preserved Greek temples are not in Greece at all: they are in Italy, at the Greek settlements at Paestum and in Sicily. I love the three great Paestum temples, beautiful and subtle structures plonked down on their flat, fertile plain like squat aircraft hangars. Structurally these temples are very simple, just stones laid flat on other stones. The Greek builders, subtle and clever though they were, knew nothing about arches – these hadn't yet been invented. They had to make do with simple posts and lintels, just like the people who erected Stonehenge. It was the Romans who in due course invented the arch. They were master engineers from the start; as architecture, as structure, Rome is indeed splendid. But, after Paestum, I find it hard to warm to the ancient Roman remains – colossal, amazing, but also hard and imperial. From the outside, the Colosseum is magnificently theatrical, truly colossal – not so much a big Globe Theatre as a Pont du Gard bent round into a circle. But inside, with its great arched entrances, its mazes of subterranean tunnels and cells, it still even now looks cruel and inhuman.

Rome

Medieval Italian cities too must have been harsh and cruel, but not on such a vast scale as Rome; it's easier to imagine the place of ordinary people within them. And some of them also reflect more attractive and more human purposes. In the Campo Santo at Pisa, it may have been the plunder of the Crusades that was transmuted into these graceful sacred structures, but the angular palaces at Florence and Siena were built to serve secular powers and to sustain that essentially Italian conception, the communal ideal. And creating campos and piazzas, outdoor places for ordinary people to share and enjoy, is something the Italians did well.

The Renaissance architects turned back to classical Greek and Roman sources, but they developed them into a new and

Florence

wholly Italian idiom. The British are much in their debt for this, for without the Italian example there could have been no Inigo Jones, no Wren, no Hawksmoor, no Kent; no Palladian houses, no Bath, no Stowe, no Edinburgh New Town.

Italian buildings are interesting because – like geometry or philosophy – they express thought and intention clearly and transparently. And when one draws Italian buildings, certain national characteristics emerge: vigour, confidence, strength, courage; ingenuity and inventiveness; hard angularity, or soft, sinuous grace; weight and solidity, but also prettiness, pattern, delicacy and colour. One discovers also a number of architectural and social forms in which Italy excels: the Roman triumphal arch and its derivative the medieval city gate; the Renaissance palace; the hill town, enclosed and fortified against marauders; the buildings clinging to steep hillsides; the narrow streets or alleys, straight or curving, sometimes little more than dark rat-runs; the houses that flank them often held apart only by stout arches and heavy brick buttresses.

The Italians were good at building tough, unadorned structures like fortresses and towers. But they were also excellent decorators, clever not only at making the structure itself decorative – as in the dazzling alternate liquorice-allsort layers of black and white marble in the cathedrals of Orvieto and Siena – but also at covering the surfaces of whole buildings with bold architectural forms: Moorish devices at Monreale in Sicily, breathtaking veneers of green and pink and white coloured marble on many Florentine churches, on the city's Duomo and on those of Siena and Orvieto. These effects are richly decorative. Indeed, buildings often *had* to be decorated, if only because they were jammed so closely together that it was hard to take them in as a whole. In a narrow street one can't step back to see a large building in its entirety: one has instead to marvel at its detail, as if inspecting nose-to-glass a picture one can't stand back from.

There is however one place where people *can* always stand back: the open space or piazza within a town, often at its very core and often in front of a great church or palace. The Italian piazza is an open-air room, a stage, a big box without a lid. It may be oblong (Venice, Volterra) or oval (Lucca), or scallop-shaped and dished (Siena), or semicircular (Naples), or pincer-shaped (St Peter's) or irregular (Florence, Massa Marittima); its surface may be level or sloping. People may enter it up ramps or down steps, or as if going onstage, through theatrical openings – tall gaps, arches, doorways. Unlike a stage, however, it usually looks good from any angle. In these admirable places, the greater and lesser surrounding buildings sit well together, as in the finest open space I've ever seen, Siena's great shell-shaped Piazza del Campo. Occasionally piazzas double as car parks, but traffic is best kept out: the piazza is a drawing-room and an open-air theatre, and it's meant not for vehicles but for people. It is *their* coming and going, their groupings and clusterings and separations, that complete the scene and make the piazza such a lovely place to be in.

Other figures too form part of this scene: figures in stone and bronze, by Michelangelo and Cellini in Florence, by Bernini on his Roman fountains, by excellent but anonymous sculptors in Verona and Mantua and elsewhere. The Italians were good not only at integrating structure and decoration but at incorporating figures on and around their buildings. Those that stand gracefully about in niches or on parapets or on top of arches in Verona or Vincenza, their balance and stance subtly emphasising the symmetry of the buildings they adorn, are enchanting and expressive. But sculptural exuberance can get out of control, as many riotous baroque façades further south demonstrate, their cornices groaning under the weight of posturing figures swaying and gesturing away like hammy actors. Those on top of the façade of S. Giovanni in Laterano in Rome, and on Bernini's Vatican colonnades, show how expressiveness can degenerate into rhetoric, and rhetoric into bombast; and the spirit fuelling this change of tone, tipping the balance, is religious.

Rome

Many of the most interesting and best-preserved old buildings in Italy are churches. They have survived because the church could afford not only to put up but to maintain durable buildings, just as it had earlier preserved – by converting them for its own use – ancient pagan ones like the Pantheon in Rome and the temples at Agrigento and Syracuse and Assisi. It's interesting to look inside these churches: to compare their interiors, spacious and austere in the north, glittering and mysterious in the south; to see the paintings and sculpture, the riches and the magic. One can observe the churches still being used for their curious rituals, and see the faces, trusting or impassive, of the people coming and going. In an Italian church, the transaction looks clear: reassurance and the prospect of eternal life being exchanged for devotion and faith, pretty much as in an English church. But Italian churches look very different from English ones. Wandering round an English church, what catches the eye is largely local history – tombs of the gentry and the military, pretty fonts and pulpits and pews with curious bench-ends, plaques recording charitable provisions for the poor. Conviction now seems fairly optional. But in Italy it isn't. An Italian church is a blast of indoctrination, full of certainty and authority and supported by dramatic and repetitive images. Churches still seem important everywhere in Italy, and not just as monuments or museums: the Church in Italy is also still clearly a going concern, powerful and dogmatic and bossy. I noticed this with mixed feelings, being interested in the buildings but put off by worship and repelled by faith.

The earlier Italian churches are beautiful but restrained: spaces to contain people, their interiors austere and unemotional, the decorative and figurative elements – paintings, sculpture, mosaics – applied rather than integral. The exteriors and especially the façades, however imposing and beautifully decorated, remain plain and structural – simple windows, geometrical patterns, tiers of arcading. But later on and further south the structures themselves become more adventurous, more flamboyant, more theatrical, and it becomes harder to separate the stonework from its pictorial or figurative content, the structure from its message. This development reaches its greatest heights of theatricality with the baroque. Its buildings, being not unlike pictures and sculpture themselves, are often particularly interesting to draw. It was in Rome that I began to notice and think about baroque architecture. There's plenty of it about. Some of the baroque façades are very pretty: curving and elastic, even rubbery, and often adorned with very lively sculpture. From the front, these façades look as solid and impressive as banks and as alluring as merry-go-round canopies – the Roman church needed this showmanship to regain its power to impress after the Reformation. The curvaceous silhouettes of these façades are magnificent, all grandiosity and bravura. But, like Italian policemen's caps, and the famous Roman matron's curly coiffure [page 120], while they stick up imposingly at the front they don't look so good from the side. For all their flowing and swirling outlines, these baroque façades are all front, all show, all presentation; from the side, which is the way one sees them while walking along the street towards them, they look thin, flimsy and meagre, like stone hoardings. Indeed, at Gravina di Puglia a great poster-like eagle stretches its outspread stone wings right across the whole façade, just as though it were a Coke ad. Buildings should be more than mere advertisements.

The most extreme and the most brilliant Roman baroque architect is Borromini. The waviness and plasticity of his façades is striking and seductive: in the weaving to and fro of his final masterpiece, the façade of San Carlo alle Quattro Fontane in Rome, the wriggling, shimmying stone almost seems alive. It's theatre, gesture, showmanship – like Bernini's splendid fountains – and it's breathtaking. At first I found it disconcerting: *should* a solid stone building look like a curtain rippling and swelling in the wind? It seemed somehow dishonest – at the very least, a contradiction. But then, I thought, why shouldn't a building look like a bit of sculpture if its architect wants it to? And gradually as I drew Borromini's work I grew to admire and love it.

In Naples and further south, angels and skeletons – life and death – begin to alternate on churches like so many carrots and sticks. The skulls, crossed bones, rib cages and complete skeletons are carved crudely but with relish. Skulls and crossbones were useful to the church: the fear of death might frighten waverers into the fold. The vigorously carved images of these handy prods, in the Via Benedetto Croce in Spaccanapoli in Naples for instance, or on the remarkable Chiesa del Purgatorio at Matera, are lively and arresting. They offer macabre warnings in brass or stone or weathered wood of imminent but still avoidable doom; but they also spur one on to get on with life while one still has the chance.

I am intrigued by the angels in Italian churches. The most primitive, the early and formalised kind in Giotto's frescos and in the Ravenna mosaics, are the best: they convey the *idea* of a winged person, not a literal depiction. In any case, Giotto's magic is in the faces and gestures: the wings are only tacked-on cardboard accessories. But later on, as sculptors

grew more interested in literal representation, angelic anatomy became more precise: by looking carefully one can see where and how the wings are fixed on and how the clothes fit around them. I noticed this first while looking at a fine rococo angel on the Ponte Sant' Angelo in Rome. Its wing-roots grew from its shoulderblades; the fine feathery wings didn't exactly look unwieldy, but rather as they might if made from polystyrene foam, big and solid but light. But would they have felt heavy, ached, swelled, perspired? The accomplished and lifelike stone pinions were interesting to draw; but Giotto's more formal ones, ideas given visible form, look less silly.

Later on, drawing the southern baroque churches in Lecce and Sicily showed me how ingeniously they'd been designed. They are very sensual, their generous curves meeting and flowing sexily into each other, their right angles sharpened and pulled out into spiky points. They are also very inventive. At Lecce, the capitals on the columns of Santa Croce and San Giovanni Battista are newly thought-up, with odd creatures and unfamiliar figures and faces instead of the stock Ionic volutes and Corinthian acanthus leaves. The façades are adorned with naked cherubs sitting on big stone beach balls, holding various props – books, instruments, crucifixes, anything – and making dramatic if conventional gestures. The effect is rich and abundant. But after a bit all this decorative baroque detail gets tedious: after drawing for a while in the hot Apulian sun I could hardly be bothered to go on peering up to find out what these thickets of squidgy carving consisted of. These famous Lecce façades are supposed to resemble marvellous displays of fruit, but they looked to me more like the Adriatic fishermen's barrows laden with their squashed-together trays of octopus and squid.

To a detached outsider, the Italian Church as an institution looks something of a dinosaur – a durable if unappealing left-over. But it's a good curator; it put up some of Italy's most interesting buildings, looks after them as splendid museums and periodically lets people in to look at them; and the priests and nuns wear distinctive habits that make the place look Italian, just as naked holy men make India look more Indian. Without the Church, Italy would look less superstitious, less irrational, but also less picturesque.

From the nineteenth century on, however, most Italian monuments are secular, their main theme unification and the Risorgimento, in the form of the myriad stone or bronze Cavours, Mazzinis and Garibaldis in every town. Political glorification, though still with quasi-religious overtones, appears at its most spectacular in the Vittoriano, the enormous and much ridiculed white Valhalla raised in the centre of Rome to the memory of Victor Emmanuel II, whose bronze dignity and metre-wide moustache is bolstered up by various quadrigas, fountains, trireme prows and angels.

But there are plenty of reminders of more recent Italian aspirations, colonial and fascist – some now harmless enough, some more sinister. The fairly harmless category includes, at the Porta Capena in Rome, an Ethiopian obelisk stolen from Axum in 1937; and, in Parma, a touching monumental group, just outside the railway station, of two noble but clearly vanquished savages welcoming a civilising pith-helmeted colonialist, hand-gun at his hip. The more sinister includes those reminders of fascism and Mussolini that were too substantial or too useful to get rid of after the regime's collapse: the post office in Naples, the Florence railway station, the grandiose bits of the Via Roma in Turin, some pretty marble landing stages in Venice, an arcaded building on one side of the Piazza del Duomo in Milan, and the Olympic Palace of the Nations – a striking arcaded block of white marble on the outskirts of Rome. The not-so-innocent precursor of all this fascist bombast was the Vittoriano. Architecturally these fascist relics vary in quality, some of them merely grandiose, others useful and practical and even elegant. Their visual worth should not be confused with their original function of making fascism look respectable. Like much totalitarian architecture, they tend to look impressive but unattractive – 'professional' and accomplished but heartless. Other reminders of fascism are more chilling, like the pretty little town of Pitigliano in southern Tuscany from which during the war the whole Jewish population was shipped firmly off, lock stock and barrel, once and for all, to the German concentration camps.

Art and Italy are synonymous. Even the colours in my paintbox have Italian names – Venetian red, Naples yellow, raw and burnt Siennas and Umbers: Italy's very earth is bound up with art. Belvedere and vista, chiaroscuro and patina and fresco are all Italian words, perspective an Italian invention. Drawing and design, activities many of us habitually separate, are embraced by the one Italian word *disegno*. This word is important because it reminds us that Italian art exists at many levels: some of it grand and exalted, some simply workmanlike. Some Italian artists are so marvellous that they make one despair: the sheer naked skill of Michelangelo's figures in the opulent and corporate-looking Medici chapels in Florence overwhelm one. But other masters, like the mosaicists of Ravenna or Naples or Pompeii, inspire one because they show what wonders can be achieved by teams of ordinary craftsmen, probably not specially gifted as individuals but properly taught and given an occasion to

rise to. There are in Italy marvels of touchingly expressive humanity like Giotto's murals in the Scrovegni chapel in Padua, whose emotional power transcends the simple means he uses. There are magical works like the stone reliefs and bronze doors of San Zeno in Verona, well observed and composed yet still with a clear-headed innocence of vision, an endearing primitiveness of touch. These humbler works remind us that art is an endeavour in which the artist is always unskilfully feeling his way, growing, never fully master; making what he can out of whatever intractable medium he's working in, and doing the best he can with his own limited powers.

San Gimignano

Italian creativity thus extends beyond the narrow bounds of fine art as conventionally defined into realms that are both more ordinary, down-to-earth and more all-pervading. For example, we now accept that architecture and engineering are almost inseparable, but the Italians were the first to demonstrate this unity. It is impossible to say whether the Galleria in Milan, the Mole Antonelliana in Turin, the tall brick towers in Bologna, even the Colosseum itself are works of architecture or engineering; they all embody that peculiarly Italian fusion of form and structure which shows that these things indeed have no independent existence. Nervi's brilliant concrete structures are the textbook example of this unity; the country's spectacular roads and bridges, viaducts and tunnels its current manifestation. This skill is not confined to engineering and architecture: design in Italy is everywhere. In the churches of Florence are many tombs with lovely graphic heraldic devices incised or inset in their marble, as simple as modern logos but subtler and more beautiful. Italians design splendid posters; but then they've been at it a long time: already in Pompeii there were election slogans painted on the walls. Stonework and brickwork, furniture, carved details, the heavy locks on chests and doors, all are done with style and vigour. It's a process that continues right up to the present day: the country that invented Futurism has also given us nippy scooters, smart cars, lovely clothes, fine furniture, good-looking office machines, digital clocks and the espresso machine – things that have indeed impinged on many people's lives. This ingenuity has stood the country in good stead: Italians still go on proudly building their own Fiats and Alfas and Lancias rather than humbly banging them out, as we do, for Ford or General Motors or BMW or Toyota or Nissan.

However much Italian life changes, many things remain as beautiful and as intensely Italian as ever: the coloured houses, in ice-cream shades of red, brown, yellow, pink and green; the flower-hung balconies from which old ladies let down shopping baskets on ropes; the washing hung out across the street. I love the Umbrian and Tuscan hills, and the hill towns on the skyline; the cypresses and umbrella pines; the little round black trees, each pinned to its shadow, dotting the yellow stubble; the landscapes patterned with vines. I love the daytime sounds of the summer heat – cicadas, frogs, crickets, swifts, buzzards, and tractors with clanking ploughs tilling the newly harvested fields – and the night-time sounds of owls as one lies naked on the bed without a sheet, hoping for a cool breeze. I enjoy the sound of church bells crashing in the belfries, and seeing them swinging wildly about in full view, not hidden away inside the towers; and I like the coffee, the good sandwiches and beer, the marvellous restaurants, the fresh pasta and parmesan and Italian wine.

Siena

I like the sightseeing: wandering about the streets of Pompeii hot but unhindered; seeing for the first time famous things that I'd known only from pictures; struggling up long flights of steps to reach a viewpoint; climbing up towers and along battlemented galleries; looking at gleaming mosaics and at intricately carved classical marble capitals and at the marvellous reliefs round the Trajan column; sitting in the Gallerias in Milan and Naples, or at a village café table; enjoying the surprising concentration of cities like Rome and Florence, places still small enough to walk around. But I'm exhilarated simply by wandering almost anywhere in Italy;

walking through arches, along colonnades, beneath statues or under arcades, along straight perspectives, on well-cut paving stones whose incised lines stop you slipping when it's wet, and noticing all the other kinds of paving – patterned cobbles, brick, dark and light stone, decoratively laid out or in rough-and-ready patterns, like old walls laid flat on the ground. I like the wall surfaces too: the worn brown bricks and the blocks of white stone embedded in them like lumps of candied peel in a slice of cassata. And I enjoy watching the everyday life: markets, kerbside stalls, groups of people chatting, young people telephoning or sitting about on their scooters, old people resting by fountains or on the long stone benches considerately built into the façades of great Renaissance palaces; the Roman dossers sleeping rough on the warm pavement gratings on autumn nights; the Roman street cats. It's pleasant being outside and yet warm, and watching other people's outdoor life – their meetings, discussions, chats, romances and rows. I like the older hotels with their venerable caged-in and rickety coin-operated lifts; and I enjoy trying to find the small cheap un-done-up pensions, their rooms looking out on to shuttered walls and rich browny-orange pantiles, their spotless interiors still left much as they always were – metal banisters round a still-grand stairwell, potted plants, a shared bathroom, no television, no drinks cabinet, not much marble and no lift – places where you go in and out unnoticed, merely hanging your key on a nail in a board, and free – *obliged*, rather – to find your breakfast somewhere else along the street.

I enjoy the fine sculpture strewn abundantly about as street decoration, as in the Piazza Navona, and the statues of scholars and artists as well as of soldiers and saints, though mainly of course of Garibaldi. But then I love all the well-observed and skilfully carved stone figures on palaces and churches, and seeing their well-caught gestures echoed in those of the real people in the street below. I like the fine equestrian statues, and the stone lions and bulls and gryphons outside the big churches, climbed on by many generations of children until the textured manes have worn smooth and acquired a polish. In Ferrara I enjoy seeing children and adults alike biking about in the traffic-free city centre, carefree and safe; and in Venice, I love being free of vehicles altogether: this, almost as much as the architecture and the water, is now that city's chief delight. I enjoy marvelling at the clothes and uniforms worn by the clergy, the military, the cadets and the police: their black, brown and white habits, blue serge, shiny leather, gold braid and pomp; and the policewomen's hair-dos. I like the tramps and their dogs, the buskers, the scruffy laid-back street musicians, the grand respectable quartets thumping away in dinner jackets in the cafés in the Piazza San Marco. It's good to see people – and not only young ones – in summer clothes that show how their bodies move (Indian sarees reveal hidden bits of body but mask their movement), or in tights just like figures by Mantegna or Pisanello. And everywhere I enjoy the Italian sense of energy, intelligence and responsiveness.

Enna

But Italy also has its disappointments. The supposedly widespread corruption and crime fortunately impinge little on the visitor; but many things that might in themselves seem desirable enough now conspire to make Italy look, even to the least observant, uglier and less Italian. They make up an alarming list of abstractions: prosperity, growth, and rising expectations; development and suburbanisation; intensifying communication, traffic and tourism; industrial farming and pollution; the universalisation of businesses, brands and logos; commercialisation and Americanisation. It's sad to find the rivers half-full of milky dishwater or dried up altogether, the streets clogged by traffic, the cafés full of other tourists, the television shoddily commercial, the splendid city centres and the pretty hill towns doughnutted by ugly development, the motorways hemmed in by warehouses and offices and plastic-sheeting greenhouses, the beautiful brick farms in the Po Valley crumbling, and the hills and mountains all topped by radio masts. I'm not keen on the new or tarted-up hotels, suddenly luxurious and expensive, with metal shutters and too much marble. I don't like being short-changed or having my pockets picked, and then becoming suspicious of people who are simply being friendly. I don't much care for the opulence of St Peter's in Rome, nor the smart but chilling architectural leftovers of fascism, nor the lurking lorry-loads of riot and drug squads with their laced-up boots, sniffer dogs and machineguns. But many of these problems are not confined to Italy; they are the price paid everywhere for success, mobility and growth, the downside of our civilised and prosperous modern life, with its glass, steel and concrete structures shooting up as irrepressibly as grass in June – indeed, replacing that very grass. Italy is just another late twentieth-century European country trying as hard as all the others to survive. Development and progress are tough and destructive; Italy has to cope with them like the rest of us, as best it can.

On balance, it does – just. Italy with its fascist past reminds one that a country, like a person, can go through a bad patch and still pull through. My time in Italy made me reflect about north and south; about being uptight or open, Puritan or Latin. Rome made me think about empire, coercion and tyranny; about history and national identity – 'Italy' as a nation didn't even exist until 1861. Being in Italy made me think afresh about faith and thinking for oneself; about theatre and spectacle; about art celebrating the Church or State's requirements, and the artist's own concerns and response to reality; about good architecture paid for, as Mussolini's Olympic village in Rome was, by an unsavoury regime. And, conversely, Italy made me think about civilisation, about creating towns and cities and a reasonably fair framework in which people can get on together decently; about beauty and creativity, art and life.

I love Italy. It's beautiful, and it makes me think, feel alive and want to draw. It's also fun. To see so much inventiveness and imaginative vigour, so many startling creative leaps and so much steady, inspired development given visible form, is exhilarating. Visiting Italy may exhaust one – looking and thinking wear one out – but it seldom lets one down or disappoints one for very long. It has preserved its astonishing past with some care, and it's trying to hold some at least of today's destructive forces at bay. Italy, like Paris, is an easy place to like: people go there in an expectant and outgoing frame of mind. I love its countryside, its towns and cities and its art – which really means its attitude to life. Italians have been creating useful and beautiful things, and having good ideas, for longer than most people in Europe. They still are. It's worth going to have a look.

Siena

Venice and the Veneto

Venice is unexpectedly different from everything you are used to. It is also unreal. You leave normal, ordinary life behind at the railway station as you step on to the vaporetto: from that moment, everything in this astonishing place, whose streets are made of water, is unusual, splendid and magical. Venice imposes its own special routines and rhythms on you. Accepting and delighting in them is part of its charm. You could be in no other city.

The city is made of lovely ingredients – white stone, warm brown brick, dark greeny-black algae, brown mud; blue or grey sky, blue and green water. Pictures, scenes and compositions unroll, unfold and present themselves on every hand: distant strips of building are spread along low quaysides; small paved piazzas are enclosed by crumbling brick walls; wherever you look there are brick and stone bridges, waterside footpaths, churches and towers and domes. And always there is the presence, seen or heard, of boats of all kinds and sizes, from lacquered gondola to cruise liner, from the boatload of complimentary bouquets for the hotel guests to the dirty-laundry boat and the refuse barge.

Venice is both romantic and practical. The romance is that of great wealth and historic importance: a sense, in St Mark's Square, where the domes and arches are oddly pointed and turban-shaped, of being at least on the threshold of the mysterious East. The romantic feeling is increased by the picturesque decadence: softened and aerially polluted brick- and stonework; sagging stone courses, no longer level; towers tilting off-vertical; the ominous refineries hazy on the skyline. The practicalities on the other hand consist of coping with and providing for the vast influx of expectant and demanding visitors, and making a good living out of them without letting Venice be entirely vulgarised or swamped by them. This is an uphill task, all the more taxing because Venice is concentrated within a small area, and its great set-pieces often get uncomfortably crowded.

Venetian sights divide themselves up into broad categories: the great obvious ones like the Rialto Bridge and the Bridge of Sighs, St Mark's and the Ducal Palace and the Salute; the smaller and more intimate scenes, the canalside alleys and the minor piazzas like Santa Maria Formosa; the quaysides and big piazzas – San Marco, the Riva degli Schiavoni, Zattere, Giudecca; and the slightly less obvious sights – those like the Frari and the old School of San Marco which though famous enough are set back or hidden from the Grand Canal. Often these places still look like Canalettos or Guardis. Then there are the minor sights, like the small churches and the canal backwaters, that one can enjoy discovering for oneself.

It would be a pity to let Venice's splendours eclipse the beauty of the fascinating cities not far away to its west: Padua with its extravagantly domed Basilica and its great Giotto murals, Palladian Vicenza with its elegantly peopled façades and its multilingual black hawkers, Mantua with its strange palaces and pretty squares, Verona with its splendid battlemented brick bridge and its operatic arena. Each of these cities has something in common with Venice itself – history, government, artistic prowess, beauty, vitality – but as they each flourished at different periods, each is subtly different and individual.

The Bridge of Sighs

Piazza San Marco

The Piazza San Marco

As you set foot in the Piazza San Marco you sense that it is one of the world's great spaces. The length and regularity of the three arcaded sides, and the exotic splendour of San Marco itself on the fourth, with its curious oriental ogee arches, its gilt glitter in the recesses, and its swelling and fluted turban-shaped onion domes, are unparalleled. When you draw it you discover that San Marco has various quirks and oddities – many different sizes of arches, some of them plain and round, others drawn up into exotic points, like those of the arcade of the Ducal Palace just to its right. Even to today's well-travelled eyes it looks, in its context of sober classical arcades and white stone, amazingly eastern, seeming not to belong to Europe at all.

The piazza is not quite as regularly laid out as it looks, for San Marco doesn't face straight down the square: its axis runs obliquely to the right, through one of the further café tables, an axis the waiters there

well understand. I sat down and drew it in early April, when not many visitors were about and the string quartets at Florian and Quadri were still playing to empty tables. Apart from the waiters and the women selling maize for the pigeons, most of the people I saw in the Piazza San Marco were standing in line waiting to be filmed in an American Express commercial.

Even at this fairly deserted time of year the interior of San Marco itself is already uncomfortably busy at most times of day. However, fewer people visit the church very early and very late in the day, and you can in any case see the whole interior in more peace by buying a ticket into the Pala d'Oro behind the altar. Looking from here up past the mosaic-covered galleries and the carved figures on the screen into the vast golden roof, dark and indistinct in the interior haze, I was reminded, far more vividly than by anything I saw in Rome, of Piranesi's ominous prison interiors.

If you walk over the Piazza to San Marco and turn right you now face the smaller but very pretty Piazzetta. The two famous columns face you, and beyond them lies the Grand Canal; Palladio's church of San Giorgio Maggiore is in the far distance. There is virtually no tide, so the gondolas are always bobbing about at quay level. The quayside here is called the Riva degli Schiavoni or Quay of Slaves; round to the left is the Paglia bridge with its famous view of the Bridge of Sighs. The guidebook-and-carnival-mask-and-straw-hat barrows are wheeled here early each morning. At the same time, the gondoliers begin to pole their craft down the small canal to their daytime mooring, to chat and spruce themselves and their boats up before their serious day's work begins. The vaporettos from the station and the bigger steamers for the Lido all stop here: it's what people come for, the heart of visitors' Venice.

The remarkable thing about these great Venetian buildings is that standing as they do at the water's edge, there are no other buildings in front of them to obstruct the view and obscure them as one sails away. As the boat moves away and they turn from close-ups into distant subjects, one sees them gradually growing smaller without ever losing sight of them. The Ducal Palace [overleaf] thus gently turns in front of your eyes from an overwhelming close-up of white stone tracery and black-shadowed arcade into the merest distant strip of white between blue water and sky. So much open space in front of such splendid buildings is unusual. In London such unbroken distant views of great buildings rarely occur – only across the Horse Guards Parade or over the Thames at Greenwich, never across the tree-filled parks. Standing by the Venetian waterside and relishing this unique sense of space is one of the city's chief pleasures.

Riva degli Schiavoni

San Marco from San Giorgio Maggiore

The Grand Canal

The first thing to do in Venice is to take the vaporetto the whole length of the S-shaped Grand Canal from the station to the Santa Zaccaria terminus near San Marco. On the way you pass under the Rialto bridge and past Santa Maria della Salute and the Ducal Palace, and an astonishing and almost unbroken succession of palace façades rising from the water. Some of these may have sunk a little low in the water, their slippery green steps may be lower or deeper than intended or may even have given way here and there, their true horizontals and perpendiculars may have gone a bit askew, but their decaying condition seldom looks desperate and is often quite attractive. More dramatic reminders of Venetian subsidence are the tilting off-vertical of the distant campaniles that one may glimpse down one of the small canals to the side. For a while at least each vaporetto trip is an enchanting experience, its progress punctuated by the short stops at the many landing stages, with the same brief and efficient routine of tying up at each before anyone is allowed off or on. There are two kinds of vaporetto, the bigger ones that ply the long, curving and wonderful Grand Canal route, and the slightly smaller and more rakish ones that take the non-scenic short cut past the docks and the railway sidings.

I've always enjoyed drawing façades: head-on full-face elevations of buildings, without depth and free of the complications of perspective. The Grand Canal offers two virtually unbroken successions of these, one on each side, from the station as far as the Customs House where the Grand Canal joins the much wider Giudecca Canal. Here and there on the way there are gaps where a small canal leads off, or where a quayside widens and an open space appears. The Piazzetta is the most spectacular of these spaces, but Santa Maria della Salute and the scene around it is the most interesting. This drawing was made after I'd sketched the Salute from the rickety wooden landing-stage opposite. This is used by the water-taxi drivers, a taciturn bunch who hang about repolishing their varnished craft as they wait for fares. The people standing about on the steps of the Salute opposite reminded me in stance and grouping of the figures Canaletto painted.

The façades of many Venetian palaces consist of variants of the same basic components: a large opening at water level, heavy and practical but undecorated, and flanked by barred windows; and above this, several upper floors, often with a central group of windows indicating a main salon and separate individual windows for minor rooms to either side. The grander façades may be surmounted by a pair of obelisks. Seen from water level, the tiled roof is usually hidden, but it is sometimes visible from a distance. Most of the beautiful bulbous Venetian chimneys have vanished. The Ca' Rezzonico is characteristic of the canalside palace in its grandest form.

In any ancient city, there is always a tension between the timeless past, the visible and fascinating history, and the duller day-to-day realities of existence – supplying, maintaining, restoring, transporting. But in Venice these activities, being entirely water-borne, have their own fascination and picturesque beauty: the car ferries and cruise liners, the vaporettos and water taxis and wine barges and furniture removal boats and the varnished gondolas all reminding one of the varied craft on Canaletto's rippling and skilfully painted water. There's no place like it.

Ca' Rezzonico

Santa Maria della Salute

Near Santa Maria dei Miracoli

Venetian backwaters

Most of the intensive wandering about that fills a day in Venice goes on, to the irritation of busy Venetians with barrows to push or big boxes to deliver, in the crowded streets and alleys that connect the Piazza San Marco with the Rialto Bridge on the one hand and the Accademia Bridge on the other. Off these routes the visitors thin out a bit, people seem more relaxed and more Italian, and you can glimpse the necessary but mundane activities that underpin the Venetian glitter – hanging out the washing, delivering groceries, emptying dustbins, scraping gondola bottoms. Visitors soon seem to discover areas they feel at home in. I liked Zattere, an area of quiet streets and slightly shabby squares, wine shops and carefully unassuming and artisanal restaurants, narrow canals with the pretty marble landing stages installed by the fascists, a church or two, a few trees and a picturesque but workmanlike boatyard.

Santa Maria formosa

In Venice it's easy to feel lost when one leaves the beaten track, because so many of its prettiest features are so often repeated: identical hump-backed brick bridges with white stone balustrades, narrow waterside alleys, dark archways into little courtyards with washing strung across them, long straight canal perspectives vanishing away between soft brick walls, backwaters that run straight and narrow for only a few yards before dividing or disappearing round a corner. If you're in an unfamiliar area you have to make an effort to remember some specific detail or risk being unable to retrace your steps. Of course you do soon find a familiar landmark and feel on safe ground again. All the same, I enjoyed wandering about Venice's minor alleys much more after I bought a good map with every minor courtyard named. The wandering was worth it, for not only the city's secondary sights – the pretty Campo Santa Maria Formosa, the Frari, San Zanipolo – but even its most insignificant details look good.

Canal near Santa Maria Formosa

Rio di San Trovaso, Zattere

The Grand Canal

Basilica del Santo

Padua

After Venice, Padua seems noisy and full of traffic. It is both a standard Italian city, modern and impersonal, with the usual beggars, traffic jams, orange buses, roundabouts, monuments and big dustbins, and also in part a historic city entered through arched gateways, its narrow streets flanked by dark and beautiful arcades. From here a few minutes' walk brings you to the remarkable Basilica del Santo, dedicated to St Anthony. This splendid building looks a little overwhelmed by its own domes. Its towers are intricately decorated. It stands in a pleasant piazza beside a fine Donatello equestrian statue, confident and masterly, of Gattamelata, a Venetian mercenary. The church was full of pilgrims, many of them young schoolchildren; a long line of them was queuing patiently to see St Anthony's Treasure, those who had got there being brusquely harried on by attendants who only need a spear or two to seem like minor

devils in a Day of Judgement. I made the drawing unharried and undisturbed from the seclusion of a café table opposite.

Later I walked back through the arcades, which by now were busy and hot, to look at the Giotto frescoes in the Scrovegni chapel. These works are remarkable for the expressive and touching humanity of the attitudes and faces, and for their simple yet concentrated compositions; both belie Giotto's apparent primitiveness. In the pleasantly green garden outside were several African hawkers who had put down their great bags of belts and handbags and were resting in the sun against a length of ancient wall; they looked very fine. I took a photograph of them, as unobtrusively as I could, but they spotted and resented it: 'Do you speak English? Parlez-vous Français? We're human beings, like you.' I felt ashamed of my rudeness in treating them merely as picturesque objects.

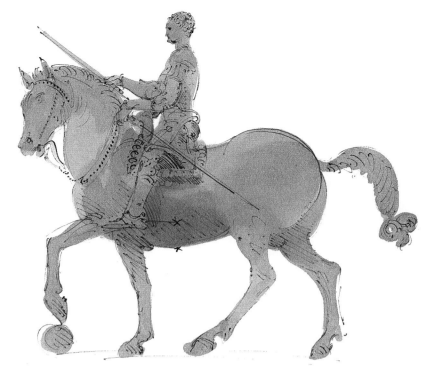

Gattamelata

Basilica del Santo

Street in Padua

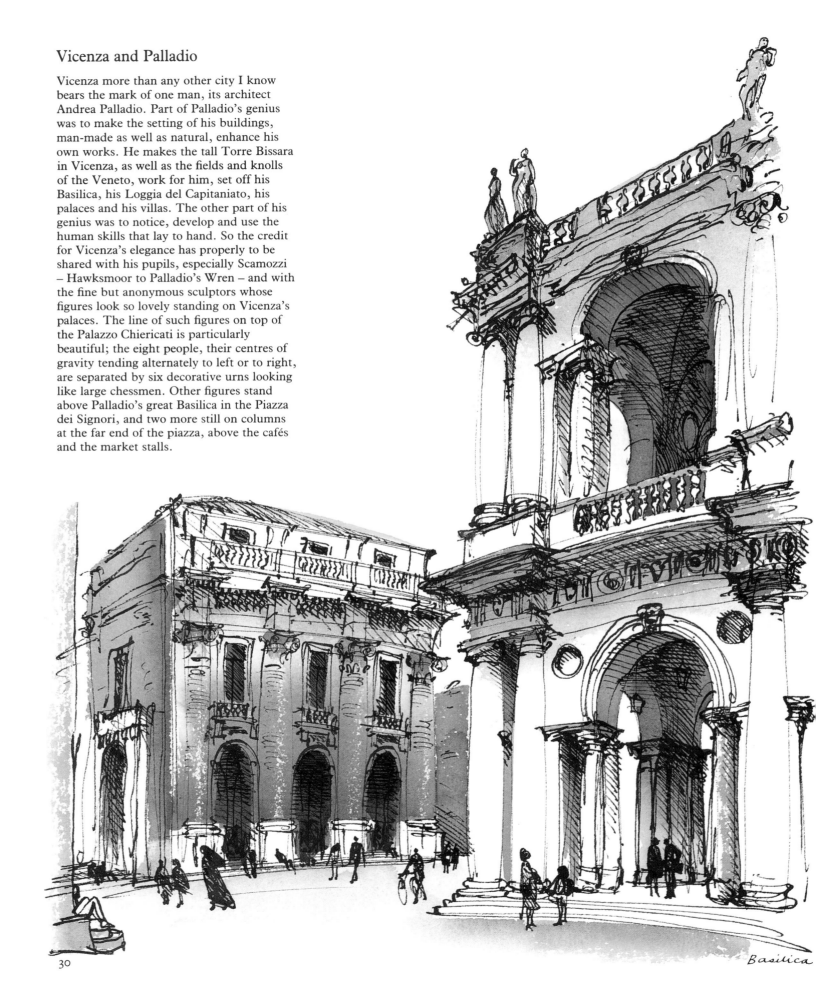

Vicenza and Palladio

Vicenza more than any other city I know bears the mark of one man, its architect Andrea Palladio. Part of Palladio's genius was to make the setting of his buildings, man-made as well as natural, enhance his own works. He makes the tall Torre Bissara in Vicenza, as well as the fields and knolls of the Veneto, work for him, set off his Basilica, his Loggia del Capitaniato, his palaces and his villas. The other part of his genius was to notice, develop and use the human skills that lay to hand. So the credit for Vicenza's elegance has properly to be shared with his pupils, especially Scamozzi – Hawksmoor to Palladio's Wren – and with the fine but anonymous sculptors whose figures look so lovely standing on Vicenza's palaces. The line of such figures on top of the Palazzo Chiericati is particularly beautiful; the eight people, their centres of gravity tending alternately to left or to right, are separated by six decorative urns looking like large chessmen. Other figures stand above Palladio's great Basilica in the Piazza dei Signori, and two more still on columns at the far end of the piazza, above the cafés and the market stalls.

Basilica

Piazza dei Signori

Palazzo Chiericati

Teatro Olimpico

Vicenza: façades and figures

Vicenza is a delightful town, small enough to walk round in an hour or two, but worth spending several days in. Its most memorable interior is the Teatro Olimpico, on whose sloping stage skilfully simplified classical buildings built in ingenious false perspective create within a tiny area a magical illusion of space and distance. Many years ago one could walk up its three wooden streets, their tall façades shrinking with each step down to waist height in the space of a few yards. Now this famous stage is more protectively taken care of, its illusions affording great pleasure to the groups of schoolchildren who enjoy its magic from in front, as Palladio intended.

While the theatre's perspectives are its most startling feature, the Palladian screen in front of them is beautiful and perfect. Its niches and cornices are adorned by several tiers of graceful figures, their attitudes and gestures easy and flowing; others stand at the back of the semicircular amphitheatre above the audience.

Yet more figures stand above the streets of the real town outside, carrying the strong uprights of Palladio's formal columns still further upwards as human forms silhouetted against the sky. Looked at in an unfriendly spirit, these beautiful figures might seem – as the Palladian façades themselves might seem – empty and bloodless, decorous but conventional, even a bit frivolous: Watteauesque. One might indeed see the whole Palladian town as a setting for a lightweight and insubstantial masque, elegant, polite and controlled rather than penetrating, dramatic or moving. But there is no doubting the style, the grace and the mastery of the whole thing, and I liked drawing both the figures and the buildings: each needs the other.

Palazzo Porto Breganze

San Vincenzo

Palazzo Porto Barbaran

While Palladio was responsible for many of Vicenza's most conspicuous buildings, he and his assistant Scamozzi also built in narrower streets and secondary places too, where their work is harder to see and may not have always survived. The Palazzo Porto Barbaran can only be looked at in close-up or obliquely; only a fragment of the beautiful Palazzo Porto Breganze remains.

Other sculptural façades are Palladian in spirit but came later; one of these, the façade of San Vincenzo by Paolo Bonin, has been added on to an older gothic church. The Redeemer and the winged Lion of St Mark at the end of the Piazza dei Signori

might have come from the Piazzetta in Venice; they look down protectively or benignly on their own beautiful piazza with more significance than Palladio's lighter and more decorative figures. They are there to add grace and elegance rather than to offer protection, and don't expect to be scrutinised too closely. The pretty figures on the Palazzo Chiericati and on the Basilica are just as essential to these buildings as their columns and arches, or the weather-cock on top of the medieval Torre Bissara.

Vicenza, like every other Italian city, has more specific and down to earth monuments as well, each put there to say something

about the Risorgimento. To English eyes these innumerable stock Garibaldis and Mazzinis and Victor Emanuel IIs all look pretty similar. We are used to individual monuments to local worthies rather than to multitudes of them all erected to the same two or three national heroes; they seem, like war memorials, both conformist and didactic. It is better to have a changeable impression, subject to revision, of what a national hero did, what a war was like, than to have idealised images of them, in period uniform or baggy trousers, stuck up for ever as immutable and shining examples, to be admired and revered without question.

Piazza dei Signori

Palazzo Chiericati

Piazza Castello

Verona: the Piazza delle Erbe and the Ponte Scaligero

Verona stands by an S-shaped bend in the River Adige. In the older part of the city are two charming squares: a thin narrow one – the Piazza delle Erbe – filled by the square white canvas awnings of its daily vegetable market, and a larger one – the Piazza dei Signori – which is grander but quieter and more reflective.

Of Verona's numerous bridges over the Adige the most singular is the Ponte Scaligero, a fortified structure built largely of brick and white stone connecting the old castle with the farther bank. It's beautiful too walk across and tempting to draw: the river looks at its best in early spring, dryish and harmless-looking, the sandy shoals beneath it providing inaccessible beaches for scavengers and wanderers. The battlements of the tall brick tower and of the bridge itself make a fine fretted silhouette; the small bastions to either side serve for hand-to-hand fighting or for sitting and reading the paper.

Over the bridge to the right is a pretty riverside path. About half a mile further upstream the great church of San Zeno [overleaf] stands between its tall campanile and a lower fortified tower. As the morning advances the Piazza San Zeno fills first with groups of schoolchildren visiting the church, and later with cars. The church is splendid inside, an airy and spacious basilica; but its greatest delights are its stone bas-reliefs and the fine bronze doors decorated with biblical scenes, marvels of concentration and expressiveness despite their early and relatively primitive technique. The view across the square towards San Zeno and its surroundings is essentially Italian: clear, simple, and strong.

Piazza delle Erbe

Ponte Scaligero

San Zeno Maggiore, Verona

Verona: piazza and arena

Verona's most interesting features are well spread about, so that as you walk from one to another you can enjoy the smaller streets and minor delights of this lovely city. In the Piazza dei Signori one's eye is drawn less to the human activity on the ground than to the bricks, stones and painted plaster that surround it, the fish-tailed battlements on the skyline and the figures that gaze down from the parapets or stand on top of the piazza's arched entrances. Grand legal and administrative buildings surround this square, but the cafés, with their flower boxes and their parasols ready to open out and blossom when the sun warms up, are friendly, touristy and delightful.

In the centre of the piazza stands a sombre Dante. There are other stone figures on the arched entrances to the piazza, figure and arch together making a dark silhouetted shape very characteristic of Verona. The colours of the piazza sit well together: warm brick and grey stone and the Italian reds and yellows of the painted plaster. The mixture of historic grandeur and cheerful day-to-day existence is a very Italian pleasure. Juliet's balcony is a few yeards away to one side; to the other are the much more interesting tombs of the noble Scaligere.

Verona's most arresting feature is the oval Roman arena. You can walk round it, taking in the details of its rough stonework, flints and bricks, and then sit at one of the cafés in the Piazza Bra and enjoy it as a backdrop, with the open square in front and the huddled houses behind it; in the streets at one's back are good and inexpensive restaurants.

It was in the Verona arena, many years ago, that I saw my first two operas, *Turandot* and *Aida*. All I can remember of them now are the town clocks chiming over the music and the partisan excitement of the many soldiers in the audience towards one or other singer. During the arias you could hear the tinkle of breaking glass as the miniature brandy bottles sold in the many intervals tumbled down the arena steps; the operas seemed to go on until about two in the morning. I think of it every time I hear *Turandot*. The great arena is still the central landmark of Verona, though inside it now looks more like an efficient auditorium than an ancient monument: performance has overtaken archaeology. But outside, with its rough and fragmentary outer wall and its massive stone arches, it still looks splendid: dramatic, and romantically ruined.

Piazza dei Signori

Dante monument

*Piazza Bra
Roman arena*

Piazza Sordello

Mantua

Mantua is a beautiful and historic town, but by no means a dying or moribund one. At its centre between the Castello di San Giorgio and the church of Sant' Andrea is enchanting succession of piazzas, the Piazza Sordello, Piazza Broletto, Piazza delle Erbe and Piazza Andrea Mantegna, this last facing a fine and spacious church by Alberti. The town doesn't look assertively prosperous but it has done very well, not out of tourism but out of plastics and electronics; from the castle one can look out over its lake and see, at a decent distance and half screened by trees, the big chemical works to which it owes some of its present discreet but evident wealth. I visited Mantua's two fine palaces, the Palazzo Ducale and Giulio Romano's mannerist Palazzo del Te; but the piazzas with their more accidental and unplanned beauty were what I most wanted to draw. In early spring the softly tinted walls were sunlit and the air was warm, though the trees were still bare. Mantua felt relaxed and full of well-being.

As in many Italian towns, the skylines are very pretty: the ample dome of Sant' Andrea, the bare Torre della Gabbia or Tower of the Cage, the crenellated Palazzo del Capitano, the funny neo-classical façade tacked on to the old Duomo, and the looming Castello di San Giorgio.

The Milanese friends who had said that Mantua mustn't be missed took me to see the grand house that Mantegna designed for himself round a circular courtyard. We also visited a good restaurant in the town; the people eating there, like those enjoying the town's pleasant and well-sited cafés, looked lively and intelligent; Mantua itself seemed provincial in the best and most vigorous sense.

Castello di San Giorgio

Sant'Andrea

Duomo

Piazza delle Erbe

Casa del Mercante

Milan and the North

The easiest way to get to Italy is to fly over the Alps; the most civilised way is to take the train, burrow underneath them and wake up in Milan. But the best way, which is also the oldest, is by road over the Great St Bernard or the Simplon passes. This is how travellers had to go in the past, and even now it's still one of the great European experiences. These routes allow one to climb out of the cool, Calvinist north into a still quite forbidding no-man's-land of rocks and torrents, snowdrifts and melting glaciers, heavy lorries and car transporters, and to pause high up in the Alpine pastures among wooden huts and cows and cowbells and milking stools and deep grass full of flowers and grasshoppers. If one then drops down past Aosta, Italy at first looks warily defensive, with fierce castles perched on every crag. But the road down from the Simplon passes pretty Lake Maggiore and its group of tiny islets, on one of which Cardinal Borromea built a grand palace and an extravagant pleasure garden. This is an architectural lollipop, a good place to spend an hour or two on a warm afternoon, but its frivolous splendour is very Italian and a foretaste of more to come. And after one has coasted on down into the great flat valley of the Po, with its intensely green ricefields, blazing acres of yellow sunflowers, jungly forests of maize, distant domed churches and striped power-station chimneys, hot empty motorways and the first roadside espresso, one knows that the journey itself has been delightful and worth the effort.

Milan and Turin with their period grandeur, their commerce and industry, and their trams, seem as much central European as particularly Italian. Turin with its monumental street plan and the fine Via Roma leading ramrod straight from the station to the palace might almost be a Napoleonic French city, apart from the glittering and inhuman Fascist section in the middle. Turin also looks more like a proper national capital (which for a while it was) than chaotic Rome does. Milan is vigorous, creative and stylish; its museums are devoted to industrial design as well as to fine art. Gothic sanctity and market-force energy face each other across the Piazza del Duomo, and the splendid Galleria stands by, uncertain which it belongs with.

I also love the third great city, the port of Genoa. It has a magnificent Renaissance centre in the Via Garibaldi, a short narrow strip consisting entirely of fine palaces; a jam-packed and battered Old Port entered through tall turreted gateways; a quayside being transformed into nautical pleasure ground; and a very grand marble railway station. But Genoa, as befits a great port, is still fairly international and cosmopolitan; Italy proper only begins further down the coast.

The remoter villages of the Cinque Terre (Five Lands), an hour or so's train journey south, are pretty well inaccessible by road. They offer a durable and heady mixture of ancient waterside buildings, newly browned German tourists and timeless crumpled rock formations covered in vines and prickly pears. The Ligurian coast is for the time being very beautiful: one should go there before too long.

Galleria Vittorio Emanuele, Milan

The Italian Alps

Even in midsummer, the first glimpses of Italy as you drive over the St Bernard or the Simplon passes are still bleak and chilly and conventionally romantic: gorges and gullies, peaks and ravines, unmelted snowdrifts crisp underfoot; fallen rocks and uprooted and tumbled-over pines that have buckled to and grown upright again, just as in Turner's sketches, and a few buildings that might or might not be habitable. The main roads are now fast and well engineered and thick with heavy commercial traffic, but up near the summits the heaviest lorries and car transporters take to the tunnel and leave the older and smaller surface roads quieter and prettier, though still needing constant repair. The border formalities are cursory, the many St Bernard dogs cuddly but stuffed, the only genuine wildlife a marmot lying dead by the roadside. A little further down on the Italian side, the streams have become rushing rivers full of icy grey water and the lorries have reappeared blinking from the tunnels. But you can climb up off the main road through pines and precipitous meadows into pleasant Alpine villages, and spend the night in a comfortable small hotel, an enlarged concrete-and-glass version replacing the original smaller and more picturesque wooden one which survives to the rear as a pretty bar. Next morning a chairlift will take you lazily up to the higher pastures and to mountain huts flying the European flag but still serving as farm shelters. The stone huts in the upland fields look very good, and even in their tumbledown state are clearly durable; they make pretty accents of grey against the mountain greenery. The newer concrete ones are duller and grow shabby more quickly. You can see the cows being milked by dairymaids on one-legged stools, and then walk back down through fir trees and a profusion of flowers, insects and butterflies. After all the car transporters, it's a magical and refreshing experience.

Paglino

San Domenico

San Domenico

Val Divedro

San Domenico

Val Divedro

San Domenico

Colle di Gran San Bernardo

Lake Maggiore and Isola Bella

The Simplon route into Italy descends through wooded ravines and beside a rushing torrent. The road is rejoined as it nears Domodossola by the pretty stonework embankments, bridges and tunnel entrances of the railway, and then becomes an ordinary fast motorway whose curves and tunnels soon take your mind off the scenery. But down to the left is Lake Maggiore, blue and idyllic, and Stresa, with lots of parking space and big white double-decker pleasure boats waiting to take you quickly across to the Borromean Islands. Isola Bella is pleasantly touristy, with plenty of cold beer and ice cream and postcards and shade at the water's edge, and a fine baroque palace only a step or two away. The palatial interiors are cold and grand, though there are more modest basement grottoes below. But its great delight is its terraced garden,

lush and jungly, and at the island's prow an amphitheatre laden with obelisks and statuary and covered in pebbles. At its base are pretty marble busts, pensively withdrawn behind dripping ferns; stone horses prance, river gods recline, bearded but naked men brandish tridents: it's all very striking but a bit camp. It was a relief to hear the terrace hedges and banana trees rustle as they were tended by real gardeners, with wooden baskets on their back, not rustics in a masque but flesh and blood. From its terraces you can look down on lawns with lemon trees and white peacocks, or out over the lake with its pretty boats and shiny hydrofoils. The Stresa shore is lined with some grand and agreeably old-fashioned hotels, their gardens full of palms; all round the lake, hazy mountains drop steeply into the blue water.

Isola Bella

Amphitheatre, Isola Bella

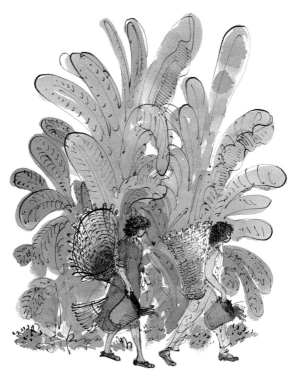

Isola Bella

Stresa

Milan

Milan's Castello Sforzesco suggests the city's medieval military strength; this century's skyscrapers display its readiness to embrace today's business climate with the technology of the present. I remember seeing one of the earliest of these tall buildings, Gio Ponti's offices for Pirelli, going up behind bamboo screens in the early fifties, sheer and metallic, vertical, impersonal and international. The Torre Velasca, a 1952 block of flats and offices, is more resolutely Italian, its oversailing upper floors and the diagonals that brace them up making one think of the Palazzo Vecchio in Florence. This building is at the very heart of Milan, a constant reminder of the nakedly structural idiom of Italy's greatest builders.

If you walk from the Piazza del Duomo straight through the Galleria you emerge opposite another famous Milanese building, La Scala: sober by comparison with the later Paris Opéra, but suitably grand and severe – its portico reminiscent of those of many grand Raj buildings in India. Orange trams trundle in dignified fashion to and fro past it.

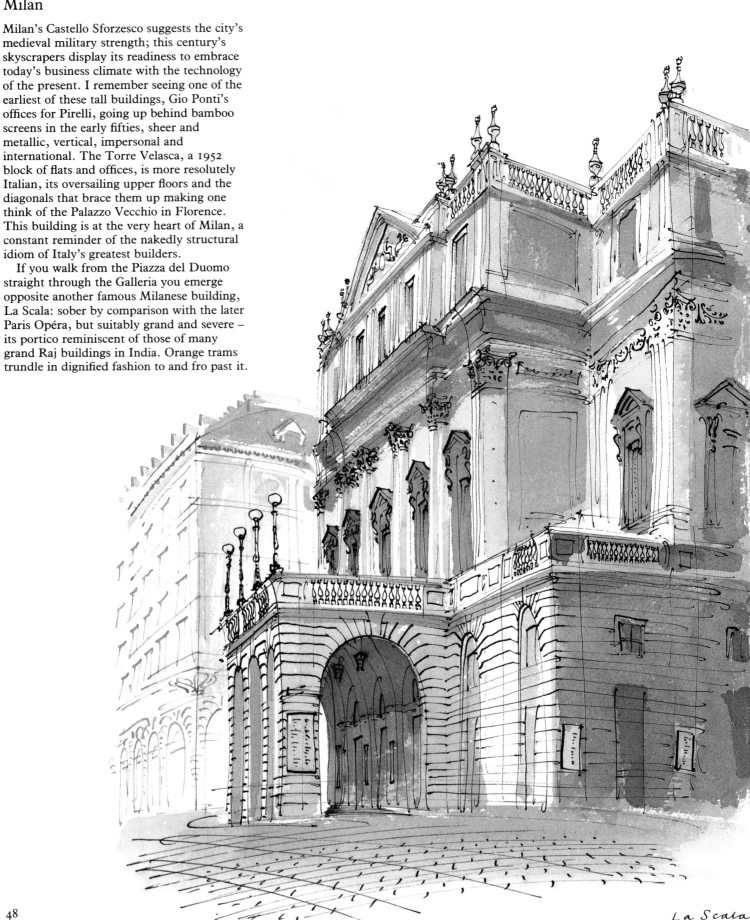

La Scala

Castello Sforzesco

Torre Velasca

Canal, Porta Ticinese

Medieval and industrial Milan

Milan's oldest and most interesting churches are within walking distance of the Duomo, to its south-east. Sant'Ambrogio is protected from its surroundings by a fine atrium, a marvellously harmonious affair of brick and stone, peaceful and withdrawn; it is overlooked by two campanili, a tall twelfth-century one and a shorter ninth-century one. Sant'Eustorgio, lower and more spread out, stands slightly apart at the edge of a small square. But the most curiously situated of these three ancient basilicas is San Lorenzo Maggiore, a fascinating brick octagon which faces a remarkable Roman remnant, a splendid classical colonnade of sixteen columns flanked by two medieval brick arches. These two structures would seem oddly assorted even without the nineteenth-century tramway laid between them, its coupled cars grinding to a stop between the statue of a classical emperor with upraised arm and the sixteen

Corinthian columns of the colonnade, its tracery of overhead cables stretched in front of the basilica's sixteenth-century dome. Parked cars add a contemporary note to this surrealistic de Chirico mixture; but I prefer the trams for their order, predictability and cleanness, and the curves, intersections, and receding perspectives of their gleaming rails: they seem the sedate but civilised servants of the city rather than, like cars, its piratical and unruly masters.

The Porta Ticinese, grandly imperial, is a Napoleonic addition to the remnants of early medieval ramparts; like the nearby canals, recently dredged and renovated, it adds a French, maybe even a Parisian touch to this beautiful and essentially Italian city. Bramante's small domed church of San Satiro, squeezed in by bigger buildings and now surrounded by traffic, has a ninth-century brick campanile. Traffic grinds or hurtles past all these buildings; a striking

Benetton poster adds a classic Italian aeroplane to the pavement scene.

Present day Milan is creative, energetic and productive, rich in history but active and vital and forward-looking. The central feature that best symbolises its busy elegance and its well-proven grasp of whatever at any period has been most modern and innovative is the Galleria Vittorio Emanuele [page 43].

Sant' Ambrogio

Sant' Eustorgio

San Lorenzo Maggiore

Porta Ticinese

San Satiro

Poster, Milan

Parma

Parma and the Lombardy farms

South of Milan the Po flows through a vast plain of flat, rich farmland, its distances broken by lines of Lombardy poplars, its horizon graced here and there by the tall striped chimneys of power stations, its fields scattered with brick farmhouses and barns. I was first alerted to the beauty of these in the fifties by the American architect G.E. Kidder Smith in his classic book *Italy Builds*. At that time, these farmsteads were still in effect isolated and self-contained communities, but as farm workers have become more mobile the farms have lost their protective and supportive functions,

and many of them are crumbling; others have been done up and gentrified. It's a pity: their lovely warm brick structures, their brick walls opened up by grand arches or pierced by myriads of intricately patterned holes for ventilation, were in their different way as important a part of the northern Italian scene as were Milan's brick Lombard-Romanesque churches.

The group of three bronze figures just in front of Parma's railway station enshrine in their *Boy's Own Paper* idiom the Italian colonial yearnings that since 1943 have been safely laid to rest. Italy was lucky to lose its

second empire as quickly and ignominiously as it did, for the loss freed it to get on with other things unhindered by nostalgia for lost imperial grandeur. Most Italians were too decent to have much stomach for the colonial spirit anyway, and would have thought it better to cultivate their own fields than to steal someone else's. Italy's true heritage, of intelligence and creative vigour rather than brute force, can be seen [overleaf] in Parma's lovely Baptistery and sturdy Duomo, with their pink and white marble and their skill at enclosing space and dividing surfaces logically and beautifully.

Near Piacenza

Farms between Parma and Piacenza

Parma

Via Roma

Turin

I took the train to Turin dutifully rather than eagerly, but instantly fell for the city, quickly finding a room with a good view quite close to the Porta Nuova station. Turin has a rather French street layout, orderly and even rigid; its straight lines and right angles make it easy to find one's way about. The characteristic feel of the city is apparent as you walk from the station down the Via Roma, a mechanically straight road that widens out halfway along to become the fine Piazza San Carlo, and ends up in front of the Palazzo Reale. A short stretch of the Via Roma was rebuilt by the fascists: its dark polished columns look a little hard and mechanical themselves; its black stonework fairly glitters with power and self-confidence and menace.

Near the Palazzo Reale are several other remarkable palaces: the Palazzo Madama, where a decorous eighteenth-century stone front has been unceremoniously and brusquely added on to a fifteenth-century

brick fortress – each slightly lowers the tone of the other – and the astonishing Palazzo Carignano by Guarini. This was the first brick-built baroque building I had ever seen, a tour de force not only in the use of seemingly unlikely material but also in the transformation of a simple rectangular façade into a wonderfully flowing and curving mass of brickwork.

Off to one side of the Via Po, but quite impossible to miss, is the striking spire of the Mole Antoniella, one of those rare architectural oddities that have by chance acquired iconic importance. It is an odd affair looking much out of proportion, like the upper part of a taller building whose base has somehow sunk into the ground. It is a notable engineering feat, but also rather a hotchpotch of steel and stone – an Italian Eiffel Tower, but less unified and coherent. Beyond it, the elegantly arcaded Piazza Vittorio Veneto stretches spacious but car-filled to the banks of the River Po.

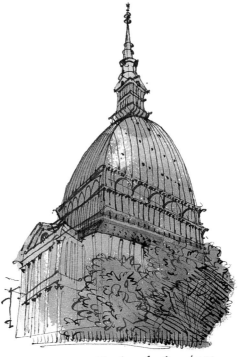

Mole Antoniella

palazzo Madama

palazzo Carignano

piazza Vittorio Veneto

Piazza San Carlo

San Lorenzo

Turin: perspectives, arches and curves

Turin's elegant arches and arcades keep people dry and cool and also look splendid. Those of the Piazza San Carlo, the first big space you see as you walk in from the station, are the most spectacular. This is a good place for a cup of coffee: the long arched perspectives are pleasantly spacious, there seems to be little tourism, you share your table with fat pigeons, and all the best shops are to be found just behind you.

At the centre of the Piazza San Carlo is a romantic equestrian statue of Emanuele Filiberto of Savoy, his steed vital and alive, snorting and pawing the ground. The Piazza Vittorio Veneto is dedicated to a newer form of transport, one for which Turin has been Italy's great torchbearer: the private car. Throughout the day, vast cohorts and phalanxes of these monsters, gleaming but motionless and inert, fill its area from end to end and from side to side in their hundreds, shimmering but inanimate, all the way from the Via Po right to the river itself.

The arcades of the Piazza San Carlo are simple and repetitive, but there are much more complicated ones inside the church of San Lorenzo, almost opposite the Palazzo Reale. This church, like the brick Palazzo Carignano, was designed by Guarini; its stunning baroque interior is almost completely hidden within a very secular-looking exterior. Inside the church the column and arches lead upwards with extraordinary ingenuity into a dome whose structure might almost have been conceived by Nervi, so elegant, logical and nakedly structural does it look.

There are humbler but still elegant arches over Turin's tramways: two or three lanes wide, sometimes leafy, and very typical of the city. By bridging the openings between the long arcaded terrace blocks they can give a whole piazza a continuity, unity and an added importance; they can also give a pleasant seclusion to the side streets screened and half closed off by their heavy columns and their hanging foliage. The gleaming tramlines beneath them converge, curve, join, separate, and vanish, just as the beautiful curving lines of Guarini's San Lorenzo do as they soar upwards, into and over his remarkable dome.

Off Corso Vittorio Emanuele II

Via Po

Piazza San Carlo

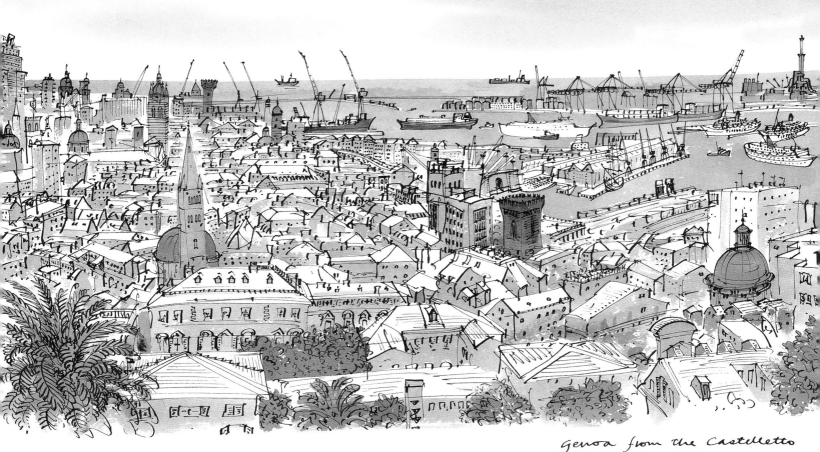

Genoa from the Castelletto

Genoa

Genoa is both an ancient Mediterranean port, its dark narrow streets deep and mysterious between high old buildings, and a new and booming modern city with tunnelled motorways running right into its heart. I made this drawing on a hot June day from the Castelletto, overlooking the fortified towers and spires and gateways of the old port, with the newer container port and its tankers and cruise ships to the right. From up here the old port looked muddled and impenetrable, dark and sweltering; it can indeed seem mysterious and intriguing and even a little menacing. One enters it through fortified gateways; its streets and alleys and churches are buried deep beneath tall blocks of housing which virtually blot out the sky; its cathedral perches on the edge of a steeply sloping piazza: its narrow pavements are patrolled in the evening by troops of police with sniffer dogs. But it probably looks more louche than it really is – at any rate, I felt safer here than in Naples. On summer evenings one can sit by the newly tidied-up quayside, or be hoisted

high into the sky by an elegant white nautical lifting device like the derrick of a monster ship, and enjoy from up there the city's spectacular backdrop of green hills. Next day, one can climb these hills effortlessly by funicular railway. At the edge of the port is the beautiful Via Garibaldi, one of Italy's most elegant streets, whose splendid palaces face each other nose to nose across a surprisingly meagre gap.

The old city was badly bombed in the war, but some of it has survived. In the middle of it is the small square of San Giorgio, where in the eleventh century the first city market used to be held. Its two handsome churches, San Giorgio and San Torpete, provided a starting point for the group of American students on the left, waiting for their professor before setting off on an architectural tour. Apart from the swelling Renaissance lines and curves of the churches, the square didn't seem particularly Italian in the conventional sense. Many of the other young people hanging about were black, their clothes and

interests as international as the Cokes and Fantas in the nearby bar, whose proprietor said he had been through the bombing. Most of the streets in the old town are extremely narrow – standing on a crossing you can look up and see only a thin cross of sky far above – and some are pretty down at heel. But, perhaps unwisely, I didn't feel at all threatened in Genoa, and it's a place I would like to go back to.

San Giorgio and San Torpete

Santa Margherita Ligure

Santa Margherita Ligure and Vernazza

The midsummer Sunday morning train south along the coast from Genoa was full of happy and noisy young people off for the day. I got off at Santa Margherita, a pleasant seaside town on whose coloured houses all the architectural decoration – quoins, courses, entablatures, cornices, window surrounds, panelling – has been expertly painted in *trompe l'œil* on to the dead flat plaster walls, as if they were theatrical flats. The quayside is pleasant despite its unending stream of cars. The farther side of Santa Margherita's harbour is occupied by masses of yachts and motor launches, some of the latter luxurious and enormous, like floating tennis courts. But pleasure boats, however shipshape and

beautiful they seem when seen individually, look en masse pretty much like litter; and all marinas look like car parks, which is pretty much what they are. From water level at least the yachts and launches are not collectively beautiful and they don't add to Santa Margherita's charm.

To escape from Santa Margherita's cars, I took the train again down the coast to Monterosso, the biggest of the Cinque Terre towns and one which I'd known many years ago. From there I caught the Gita or round trip launch to its nearest neighbour, Vernazza. In earlier days the Cinque Terre, or Five Lands, were inaccessible by road and you could only get to them by train or by boat. There are now some roads down

to these isolated villages but the coast itself still looks fairly untouched, with terraced vineyards climbing steeply up above the fantastically crumpled cliffs. The motorway is safely out of earshot some miles inland. Vernazza itself, even in mid-June, compromises skilfully between preserving the character of a pretty village – church, castle, small beach, cacti-fringed cliffs – and meeting the simple needs of the mainly German visitors for rocks to sunbathe on, a beach to swim from, and shady places to eat, drink and sleep in. Vernazza's houses are old and beautiful; it's peaceful and free of traffic. Any place without cars, however primitive, is preferable to any place, however chic, with them.

Vernazza

Portofino

Portofino is squeezed in a cranny of the green Ligurian coastline, compact, brightly painted and exquisite, and rich and expensive, its quayside a curving St. Tropez. It's remarkably pretty. Looking down from the castello high above it, the lines of boats no longer look like litter but more like bath toys, white and gleaming, the newest and grandest of them sharply pointed like paper darts or missiles. Nothing in Portofino, not even its wealth, has got out of control – the houses that have spread on to the surrounding hills are well hidden by trees, the cafés and restaurants and boutiques on the quay are impeccably smart, the women beautifully dressed. The boatmen playing cards there in the afternoon, brown and weatherbeaten, their jeans bleached, look chic and prosperous.

By far the biggest and smartest boat in the harbour was black and sleek and rather sinister, the kind a Bond villain might use. The girl at the Armani boutique told me it belonged to Valentino, a rival designer. Even at midsummer, the last boat back to Santa Margherita leaves at six and Portofino suddenly empties and dies down, the curving quayside left to a few locals. Portofino ought to look ruined by all its cash and commerce and new paint, but I thought it a pretty, lively and charming place. If you follow the hillside path past the castello and on through ferns and pines to the point, you come to a terrace by a lighthouse, high above the sea. From up here, it looks calm and tempting: a fishing boat bobs lazily about far beneath you, the water is a deep clear blue, the fast launches are away out of sight. This is how the Mediterranean ideally ought to look.

Portofino

Portofino

Florence and Tuscany

Siena has always been my favourite Italian city; but Florence is the big and overwhelming one. I hadn't stayed there since I was a student, when I'd never much liked it because it made me feel ignorant. It wasn't just hot and crowded; it was the daunting capital of culture and civilisation. But on a recent February visit it was almost empty, apart from bemused groups of Japanese, troupes of young American college students, and the pavement Africans selling handbags and umbrellas. This time I began to understand the city's structure – the old square Roman town with its arena's ground plan still discernible near the Arno, and the narrow angular medieval streets that twist and turn and suddenly deposit you at the feet of Florence's overwhelming marvel, the Duomo. I grew to love its palaces – subtle Rucellai, overbearing Strozzi, flamboyant Pitti – and to relish the differences between the various churches, and to wonder at the great imaginative leap that made possible the grouping of the Foundling Hospital and SS Annunziata and led on to the whole art of Renaissance town planning. I grew to like the Boboli Gardens and the Belvedere, with their views [overleaf] across a city still even now dominated by medieval church and *comune*, Duomo and Signoria; and to wonder how the enterprising but shrewd Florentines have contrived to keep their lovely surrounding hills so green and un-built-up.

In Siena, nothing's level; its streets plunge and twist; its piazzas slope steeply; its greatest glory, the Piazza del Campo, is built around a shell-shaped bowl suspended hammock-like between two hilltops. This city is smaller and more intimate than Florence, yet Siena seems to dominate its own beautiful landscape, much as the Simone Martini painting of a hill town in the Palazzo Pubblico does. Most of Siena is built of warm orange-red bricks made of the local clay – of burnt sienna, in fact. The houses face one another over even narrower streets, their bulging walls often held apart only by arches and buttresses; building lines are subtly angled to follow old and almost imperceptible changes of direction. The shapes of these Sienese buildings are strong but not rigid; walking between them is like walking through sculpture. But most Tuscan towns are fascinating. Lucca and Pisa, Volterra and Massa Marittima too, with their towers and gateways, churches and piazzas, are beautiful just to walk about in; San Gimignano, despite the plastic armour and the stuffed boars' heads, is no mere tourist trap; Monteriggioni is a small-scale vision of perfection.

Tuscany is much loved by the English, and it's true that in summer there are plenty of us about, looking at pictures and putting on operas and running summer schools. But if Tuscany were really Chiantishire there would be no point in going: it would be insufferable. In truth, the influx is from the north in general; and with good reason. In Tuscany the landscape is at its most 'Italian': the pretty hills criss-crossed by white roads, patterned by long lines of vines, dotted by thin cypresses and round blobs of oak; the hillocks are crowned by isolated farms and castellos. It's an idyllic landscape, like the backgrounds in Tuscan paintings; in the late afternoons the warm air becomes hazy and separates, as if with an airbrush, the various hilly skylines, making them recede one behind the other, each layer paler and mistier than the last, until eventually they vanish into the invisible distance. No wonder people think Tuscany is beautiful.

Duomo, Florence

Florence and the Arno

The Arno flows through Florence, brown and swirling and rather menacing in spring, separating the old Roman city on the flat ground from the pretty hillside palaces, gardens, churches and fort on the south bank: places that either require or exploit rising ground, and offer fine aerial views back across the heart of Florence towards the more distant hills to the north.

Of the various Arno bridges, the most beautiful is the Ponte Santa Trinità, its three wonderfully low and wide arches echoing its name. Two graceful stone figures stand at either end. But the Ponte Vecchio, or Old Bridge, is the one everybody thinks of first. It's far more of an eye-catcher. The shops and houses crammed on to its arches, though smart and well restored, still half-suggest the densely packed medieval streets, now cleared away, that used to lie just to the north of it. Even in late February when many of the jewellers' shops and other boutiques are closed, the Ponte Vecchio symbolises Florentine luxury and wealth, but also its tougher, more disreputable aspects – lively and tarty, it is also a place

for pick-ups and pickpockets. For most of its length the shops shut off or mask the views of the river, but at the centre is an open space with a fountain from which you can look out over the Arno and the remarkable buildings along its banks, some fortified, others elegant, others historic, others nondescript. The arches visible on the farther side of the bridge carry the Corridoio Vasariano, the secure covered corridor that links the Palazzo Vecchio on the north bank with the Pitti Palace on the south. The Palazzo Vecchio, whether seen from head on or at an angle, is Florence's most memorable secular building – a commanding and impregnable stone cube with a tall bell tower, the crenellations almost the only decoration. It's a tough, austere, no-nonsense building, built more to survive and impress than to delight. But nearby Orsanmichele, originally as practical as a mere grain storehouse can be, has ended up as a thing of beauty, richly decorated and dripping with sculpture.

The Pitti Palace is all impressiveness, all façade, its wings framing and increasing its

immense breadth. Behind it are the pretty Boboli Gardens with their statuary, their pleached alleys, their fountains, their belvedere, all climbing the slopes of Florence's nearest hill. From the terrace at its top you can see a further upland skyline with olives and cypresses and a towered castello, just as in a Tuscan painting.

The Ponte Santa Trinità leads over to a part of Florence, also low-lying and flat, where you can still see the small ground-floor workshops – of cabinet makers, metal workers, framers – that used until they were crowded out to be a lively feature of the city centre. There is an arty and Parisian left-bank feel to this area, with its many small restaurants, its American mature students, and its slightly self-conscious street market in the Piazza Santo Spirito in front of Brunelleschi's elegant church. Santo Spirito's cool grey interior is calm and splendid, the essence of the Florentine renaissance. Another nearby church, Santa Maria del Carmine, contains the remarkable frescoes by Masaccio of the *Tribute Money* and the *Expulsion of Adam and Eve*.

Ponte Vecchio

Ponte Vecchio

Santo Spirito

Orsanmichele

Boboli Gardens

Palazzo Vecchio

Palazzo Pitti

View from Boboli Gardens

Palazzo Rucellai

Bargello

Palazzo Medici-Riccardi

Via de' Bardi

Palazzo Pitti

Via del Proconsolo

The palaces of Florence

Even the grandest Florentine palazzi are mostly squeezed or slipped into place between and opposite other buildings, forced to fit into a gap rather than standing splendidly apart. So they look out on to pavements and passers-by rather than on to protective forecourts and distant prospects; their own courtyards are small, internal and hidden, not large external buffer zones. Only the Pitti Palace stands grandly back from its surroundings, and even then not very far back – only a stone's throw across the street from a line of fairly run-of-the-mill shop-fronts.

The Palazzo Rucellai, a magically delicate façade designed by Alberti, standing at the edge of a tiny triangle of open space, is the hardest of them all to step back from; you have to look obliquely across the street at the fastidious and understated rustication of its storeys of arches. The Palazzo Medici-Riccardi is more assertive, standing bold and dark under its beetling cornice on the

Via Cavour just where this much wider road changes direction, so that no one looking along it can miss the Palazzo's heavy dominance: it brazenly hogs the view.

Over the river, the Palazzo Bardi stands on the narrow and rising Via de' Bardi. It, too, makes the most of a bend in the street where despite its size and strength and elegance it could easily have escaped notice. The Palazzo Pazzi in the Via del Proconsolo however has no such advantage, standing on a straight street and distinguishing itself instead by the bold patterning of its heavy rustication and by its immense arch. A little further along the street is the medieval Bargello, distinguished from the five later palaces mentioned above by its skyline – the others all have level and unemphatic roof-lines, whereas the Bargello is battlemented, its picturesqueness further increased by a tower. Along with the stepped campanile of the abbey church of the Badia opposite it, the Bargello's tower is one of the central

landmarks of the older Florentine skyline, overtopped only by the Palazzo Vecchio and Brunelleschi's magnificent Duomo.

The Palazzo Vecchio dominates not only by its size and height, but also by virtue of the fine open space around it, the Piazza della Signoria, which allows one to see the building not just as a façade but as a solid object, strong and commanding, subtle and beautiful, the powerful symbol of Florence's secular majesty. It can be walked round, examined, stood back from; and you can go inside and see the courtyards. These surprised me; I'd stupidly supposed that any building so stout-looking would be solid through and through, like a lump of cheese. Both palace and tower have projecting upper storeys, like the Torre Velasca in Milan; these might have made it look top-heavy, but instead make the lower parts look sparer and more elegant and the upper parts more interesting and more individual, unmistakable on the city skyline.

Palazzo Vecchio

The churches of Florence

The great and beautiful Florentine churches are distinguished from each other almost as much by situation as by their individual style. San Miniato al Monte looks out from the brow of a hill, Santa Croce surveys an open and splendid square. Santa Croce's interior is broad, vast and magnificent. The coloured marble of its facade is subdued by comparison with those of the Duomo or San Miniato or Santa Maria Novella, but it is still very pretty. To its right you can just see the flattish dome of Brunelleschi's Pazzi chapel, smaller of course than his Santo Spirito but simple, clear-headed and perfect in its conception. Santo Spirito is set on a stepped plinth amid a higgledy-piggledy array of rubbish bins and parked cars; there is a morning market in a little square to the left, pleasant but a bit folksy. San Lorenzo is surrounded by touristy market stalls; Santa Maria Novella faces a sunny and grassy piazza occupied by obelisks and old men; the Santissima Annunziata overlooks its own extremely grand and splendidly planned piazza with the Ospedale degli Innocenti (Foundling Hospital) on the left, two fountains and a fine equestrian statue in the middle, and a splendid arcaded building on the right. It also has a distant view of the dome of the Duomo [page 6]. The Duomo itself faces quite an open space occupied by its octagonal baptistery and its tall campanile or bell-tower, while its enormous aspidal bottom settles itself down among taxi drivers and an enclosing apron of lower buildings, minor but fascinating, at the very heart of the city. One of Florence's many surprises is the way its narrow streets, further darkened by the greatly projecting eaves, suddenly half-turn a corner and open on to the sometimes rather cramped space round the back of the Duomo. In this space, the Duomo's own rigidly logical and intellectually conceived ground plan co-exists beside the older, freer but ineradicable building lines of the earlier medieval town. Most of the other churches have their own cloisters or chapels or gardens at hand, but the Duomo stands in total isolation, surrounded only by the life of the pavement: instant portraitists, poster and handbag hawkers, taxi drivers, docile groups of visitors, and an irrepressible beggar tootling a toy trumpet.

Baptistry

Santo Spirito

Santa Croce

Duomo

Monteriggioni and San Gimignano

In the pretty Tuscan landscape south of Florence are two many-towered settlements, one small and compact, the other bigger and more spread-out. Monteriggioni is hardly more than a fortified wall enclosing a small church and a square of houses. The village is approached uphill through some of the beautiful vineyards whose patterned slopes are such a lovely and recurrent Italian feature – the growing vines, black and bare in February, following the clearly defined lines established by the white concrete posts at either end and the intermediate wooden uprights that hold up the taut wire: a straitjacket pattern of parallel straight lines if you imagine it seen in plan, its rigidity softening however as the straight lines of the vines are traced over the unevenly curving shapes of the hillsides. Monteriggioni is entered through two stone arches: the interior piazza is modest but perfect of its kind, and rigorously unspoilt.

San Gimignano isn't entirely given over to tourism. A fruit and vegetable market survives at the foot of two of its towers; not all the shops sell plastic armour and torture gear; out of season at least there are more locals than visitors. I made this drawing on a showery February day and was glad every now and then to be able to shelter within the big communal archway on the right, thoughtfully provided with metal chairs.

San Gimignano looks from a distance like a rural Manhattan. It seems much more dependent than Monteriggioni on its visitors, its doorways hidden behind peasanty pottery and postcard stands, tusky and bristly stuffed boars' heads, piles of film and earthenware platters. But these are minor irritants by comparison with its astonishing profusion of tall towers, possibly defensive in purpose but alternatively thought to have been used to hang up the town's valuable dyed cloth, much as the weather-boarded towers on the beach at Hastings were used to dry fishermen's nets. Either way, these explanations shows medieval San Gimignano to have been energetic, determined and resourceful. You can climb to the top of the tallest of its towers and look out over the beautiful surrounding hills. These are well cultivated, with lines of vines stretching as far as you can see, and new roads and new houses dotted about here and there but not harming the landscape. But from up here the other lower towers look duller and insignificant, some with mere trap-doors in their roofs, others topped by little terraces where the owners can have an undisturbed aperitif as they catch up on weeding the stonework. San Gimignano's towers, like many other awe-inspiring objects, look most impressive from below, standing like rigid pointers against the clouds. From above they just look like responsibilities.

Monteriggioni

San Gimignano

Castello di Montepò

The Castello di Montepò

Tuscany between Grosseto and Lake Bolsena is rural and wild, with magnificent upland distances and occasional dramatic rocky outcrops. On one of these, Montepò, near Scansano, stands a remarkable building in which are happily combined the characteristics of fortress, stronghold, palace and country house: magnificent from afar, forbidding from below, commanding, all-seeing and patrician from within. Its own many-tiered terraces look out over a beautiful landscape of cornfields, sheep pasture, vineyard and olive groves and woodland, dotted here and there with the scattered tenant farms between which the estate is parcelled out. This landscape is very different from that around San Gimignano, with more oaks and wheat but fewer vines and cypresses, and also with

fewer villages – here there is a sense of stepping backwards into a lonelier epoch. The receding sloping harvest fields with their lines of straw, and the distant tree-dotted skylines, are very beautiful. In certain lights the nearer clumps of woodland may look rather like English parkland. But whether in the grey morning light or in the blazing midday glare, or towards sunset when the sky yellows and the trees turn black, the vast expanse of further hills looks very Italian. From below or afar, the terraced eminence on which the building stands looks almost as architectural as the house itself: rocky, angular, hard and unyielding, though softened by the small trees. But from above, one sees only the woodland and the crops, the hedges and the white roads beneath the distant hills.

Montepò

Via Galluzza   *Via del Porrione*   *Via di Citta*

Siena

Siena, like San Gimignano, stands on a hill, or rather three hills, so its steep streets twist about and its lovely buildings come at you unexpectedly. The roof eaves don't project as far over the street as they do in Florence, so the Sienese houses look simpler and more solid. The subtle changes of direction of its lines of houses, which make it hard to distinguish between slight angles and gentle curves, reappear in the D-shaped wall of houses around the great Piazza del Campo. Walls are often off-vertical and have a past – brick arches which have been filled in, festoons of old cables, ancient shutters. Walking these streets is a delight. There are no pavements but little traffic. The shops have been designed to respect rather than to do battle with the street facades: old and new do each other good.

Siena's tall houses are often separated by the narrowest of alleys and some have to be held apart by complicated series of brick arches; stone, plaster and brickwork the colour of burnt sienna here merge into a dark warm dusty unity of colour. The nine-arched Via Galluzza is the most curious of the many narrow little streets that drop away behind the Duomo down one of the city's steep slopes. The feel of the city changes as you walk from the commercial and administrative buildings near the Piazza Matteotti; past the exquisite older Piazza Salimbeni, surrounded by historical buildings from different periods, one to each side; on round the splendour of the Piazza del Campo; and up into the old streets near the Duomo. In the walls and columns of this remarkable building and on its tower [page 86], layers of black and white stone alternate. This gives a striped effect as of liquorice allsorts even on the plain flat areas, and – where the stones are cut into three-dimensional shapes – a complicated and dazzling effect not unlike a Bridget Riley painting. The Duomo has a marvellous interior, with a pulpit by Nicolo Pisano and a remarkable pictorial pavement of inlaid or intarsio marble. The Duomo is not cut off from life, as if in a quiet close; facing it just across the piazza is its own busy hospital.

Caffe
BATANI

48

16

Via Galluzza

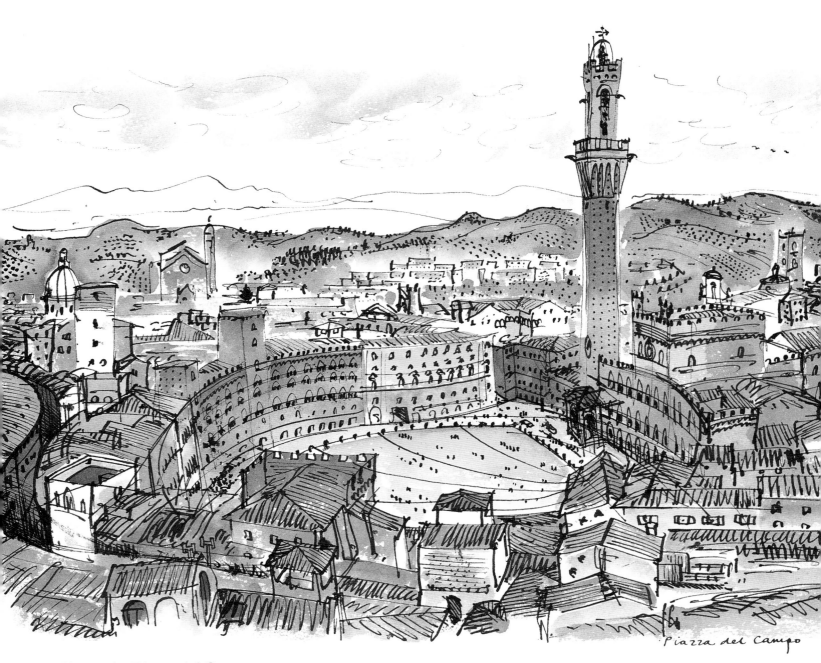

Piazza del Campo

Siena: the Piazza del Campo

Next to the Duomo in Siena is its own museum, the Opera del Duomo, which displays some fine if time-ravaged statues by Giovanni Pisano, rescued from the Duomo's façade, and many interesting early Sienese paintings including Duccio's *Maestà* altarpiece. The Opera del Duomo is the remnant of a hugely ambitious plan to build a much larger cathedral, begun and then quickly abandoned because of the plague in the fourteenth century; the existing Duomo, which seems immense enough, occupies what would have been merely the transept of the abandoned one. Once inside the Opera del Duomo one can climb up to an alarmingly high and windy brick terrace, and from here look down on the bricks and

tiles of the whole city of Siena. The most interesting feature of all this is the aerial view it affords of the magnificent Piazza del Campo and of the swirling curves of its surrounding streets. This is where the Palio horse race is held; but I love the piazza best in its normal everyday state, with Siena's own townspeople crossing and recrossing its shallow shell-shaped brick bowl, enjoying its cafés, and looking up at the brickwork of the great Palazzo Pubblico [overleaf].

I drew the Piazza del Campo many times, half hoping to discover a 'best' viewpoint, but the piazza looks good from anywhere. In drawing it I began to notice other unsuspected subtleties: to see for instance how cleverly the house façades are made to

share common horizontal features in order to disguise their various unrelated floor- and window-levels; how tense, subtle and taut the curving sweep of these buildings really is, by no means the simple semicircle that it seems at first but rather a rounded trapezium; and to realise also how cunningly at the end of this long unbroken curve the lines lead on and away and slightly outwards, forming as it were the serifs of a Roman capital D rather than being chopped off short at the corner as a sanserif D would be. It's not necessary or helpful to try to disentangle accident from design in these happy nuances: whether achieved consciously or willy-nilly, the effect is satisfying and delightful.

Piazza del Campo

Palazzo Pubblico, Siena

Four Tuscan towers

Italian towers were used for many purposes: for hanging bells in, for frightening off possible marauders, for retreating into in times of trouble, for upstaging rivals, for hanging up lengths of dyed silk to dry in. Towers were by nature conspicuous and, whether by intent or not, drew attention to themselves – they couldn't fail to. They could be seen when no other part of the building beneath is visible, and from afar; as landmarks, they enabled one to orientate oneself; the grander ones, such as the great towers of Venice and Florence, Bologna and Turin, served like skyscrapers as symbols of wealth and might. Towers could be round or square, brick or stone, austere or decorative, plain or striped, blunt or pointed, upright or leaning; firm foundations were advisable but not essential. Siena's Duomo has the tallest of the stripey ones, San Gimignano the barest but most profuse, Lucca the most varied, Pisa the best-known – a national emblem.

Leaning or not it is still a very beautiful structure, clear and inspired in conception and perfectly realised: an idea of staggering simplicity. Here the tiers contain the same number of columns all the way up. Its Pisan Romanesque decoration stops it looking bare but doesn't obtrude. It's interesting to see the complexity and determination of the current endeavours to shore it up or at least halt its increasing tilt. But the Leaning Tower's true importance is as just one element in a remarkable architectural whole. The Piazza del Duomo or Campo dei Miracoli [overleaf] comprises three more great buildings, the Duomo, the Baptistery, and the Campo Santo or cemetery, which do indeed add up to more than the sum of their parts. Whatever their purposes, silhouetted against a pale sky or white against a blue one, these are beautiful and exhilarating achievements of thought and ingenuity.

Siena, San Gimignano, Lucca

Pisa

Campo dei Miracoli, Pisa

Piazza dell' Anfiteatro

Lucca

Lucca is a charming city, packed with pretty churches and tall towers, and insulated from its ring road by its splendid encircling ramparts which carry an avenue of tall plane trees, their long bare trunks cool and yellow and vanishing up into the dark foliage; you can hire a bike and cycle round the city beneath them. Lucca was colonised by the Romans in 200 BC; the oval piazza in the old city occupies what was once a Roman amphitheatre. It's well provided with cafés but never seems overcrowded. People get in and out of the piazza through four big arches.

Of Lucca's many churches, the most striking externally is San Michele in Foro, whose arcaded façade in Lucca-Pisan style – blind arcading, ornately and geometrically decorated – towers high above the nave behind it. I'd assumed this free-standing façade, rising unsupported high above the nave at its back, was a precursor of that flamboyant showmanship later to become familiar in baroque façades. But it wasn't – the nave itself was meant to have been higher. The lowest arcade, restored, is in the manner of those of the Leaning Tower and the Duomo in Pisa, but its upper aracades are much more richly decorated.

The church stands in a lively piazza in the busiest part of town surrounded by cafés and ice-cream bars and Luccans hurrying to market. There is also a cathedral with a beautiful tomb by Jacopo della Quercia; and there are many more of the Luccan towers. The old Roman city just south of the Piazza dell' Anfiteatro established the rigid street plan which has remained as Lucca has spread. Of Lucca's various tall towers the oddest is that of the Casa Guinigi: if you climb it you can enjoy a panorama of the city from the shades of a pleasant group of trees, high above roof level. At your feet stretches a vast expanse of red-brown tiled rooftops, separated here and there by the deep gullies of the narrow streets with their yellow painted walls. Many towers, of churches or free-standing, rise from this sea of tiles, and some contractors' cranes. Beyond them to the north is a stretch of green where the tree-covered ramparts encircle the city, protecting it from its ring road; further away still rise successive ranges of hills, the nearer ones round and wooded, the further mountains bare and grey in the haze.

Casa Guinigi
San Michele in Foro

Catureglio, Diecimo and the Ponte della Maddalena

Parts of the beautiful Tuscan landscape are still relatively little known. North of Lucca the River Serchio flows through a wide and prosperous plain, rather too thickly dotted with new red-tiled roofs. Beyond this plain rise the Apuan Alps, steep and thickly wooded and enchanting. Their valleys conceal villages, fine bridges, disused mills, churches, farms and remote but still active stone quarries; and, at Diecimo, a tiny church with a perfect tower, tall and square and still vertical, the number of arched openings increasing as the tiers ascend.

On a wooded hillside near Borgo a Mozzano an old stone house, originally a gaunt and fortress-like cube but later widened and domesticated, stands between stoutly terraced olive groves and a group of smaller buildings – barns, sheds, workshops, houses, water-mills – with

which it once formed a self-contained rural community. Catureglio is secluded, the only sounds those of dripping fountains and croaking frogs; big slugs embrace oozily on the trunks of the pines. Nothing but well-wooded hillsides and barer and more distant mountains can be seen from it. But it is not entirely cut off from the present day. Parachutists and hang-gliders float from the steep hilltop above it; very occasionally a distant car grinds invisibly up through the deep woodland on the hillside opposite.

The Serchio is bridged by the graceful Ponte della Maddalena or Devil's Bridge, a narrow and remarkably delicate structure which has retained its fragile beauty despite having had to find room for a railway line. Luckily it's too narrow for cars. I wondered whether its builders had arrived at its shape by instinct or had somehow drawn it out.

Diecimo

Ponte della Maddalena

Massa Marittima

Massa Marittima, Terme di Saturnia and Pitigliano

Massa Marittima is a beautiful hillside town, quite small, at whose centre the Piazza Garibaldi is flanked by two magnificent Romanesque palaces and the Duomo. It is an enchanting combination of the monumental, the grand and the ordinary – a good place to abandon your car, pause, look about, and have lunch. A few miles north is the curious and surrealist landscape of Larderello, seething with the escaping steam and hidden energy of its hot springs, which are tapped and turned into electricity by its power station: its slightly menacing shiny pipes, snaking over the hillsides, and its cooling towers are assertively of the present day. There are more hot springs, smaller but untapped and easier to see, at Terme di Saturnia beyond Grosseto. Here the warm water surfaces as a narrow stream, running swiftly between grassy banks and bamboo thickets until, flowing over a low limestone cliff, it makes a pleasant but undramatic waterfall. The almost naked bodies of the bathers and the grey rocks make Terme di Saturnia look pagan and timeless.

A little further inland is the small hill town of Pitigliano, best seen from across the gorge of the Fiume Lente; from here its rocky cliff-top site can be seen at its most dramatic. Pitigliano's recent history too has not lacked drama. This is the inoffensive-looking town from which, in the war, the Christian fascists despatched to Germany the entire sizeable Jewish community.

Twenty miles to the west, and just into Umbria, is a larger hill town, Orvieto. I didn't yet know of Pitigliano's wartime history when I saw, on the façade of Orvieto's cathedral, the macabre fourteenth-century bas-relief of the Day of Judgement. But its hapless naked figures, pitiable and tormented, huddled and crouching, reminded me of the terrible wartime photographs of the concentration camps.

Larderello

Terme di Saturnia

Orvieto

Pitigliano

Umbria and the East

The Adriatic or eastern side of Italy is emptier, further away, less developed, and a bit duller than the western or Tuscan side. Venice is its one really extraordinary city, whereas on the west there are three: Genoa, Rome and Naples. The Adriatic side is less visited, by the British at least, than Tuscany; maybe people tend to hold the right-hand side of Italy in reserve, as someplace to go to another time. But as Italy grows busier, this relative dullness is becoming a virtue. Here and there the coast is beautiful, and inland are many lovely smaller towns and villages and an unspoilt landscape.

Ravenna was once important as the gateway to the Eastern Empire, and it is still a busy working port. It is a famous place of pilgrimage for its fine Byzantine basilicas and their lovely glowing mosaics, each one a triumph of imagination and order. It is strange to stand outside Sant' Apollinare in Classe while one's mind is still full of the calm mosaic images of sheep, trees and saints inside, and see the heavy motorway lorries placidly crossing the flat green landscape. Nearby Ferrara, surrounded by vast fields of fruit trees, is a city of bicycles, free of traffic; it has a fine castle, a cathedral and many palaces and galleries. It seems little visited by northerners, yet it is the perfect minor Italian city. Bologna certainly *is* famous, bigger and full of learning, leftwing politics, brick towers, trade fairs and displays of ham.

Umbria is in the very middle of Italy, its navel as it were, and, as the only wholly landlocked region south of Lombardy, it has no beach resorts. The Umbrian towns and villages are markedly different from the Tuscan ones just to their north-west; stonier, darker, a bit harsher. Perugia has a fine city centre, with arched alleys and a splendid Priors' Palace whose bronze lions and gryphons, heavy with pigeons, glare down on the piazza. I went to Assisi with some misgivings, wary of the prospect of much holiness, devotion and pilgrimage. There was indeed some of each but it was extremely hot and the misgivings melted away. The frescoes by Giotto and others in the basilica are remarkable; there is a pretty duomo and a fine castle overlooking the whole town; on the main square the delicate Corinthian façade of the Temple of Minerva, long since converted into a church and looking remarkably out of place alongside the medieval arches and tower, is wholly splendid all the same.

The Marches have one unforgettable city, Urbino, full of history but alive with agreeably youthful and scatty Italian students. The town is enchanting: steep hilly streets, arches, arcades, terraces, vistas on to seas of pantiles, good cafés, Federico da Montefeltro's pink Ducal Palace dominating the whole scene. Around it spreads a wonderful landscape of rounded and patterned hills, each – when the weather is right – surmounted by its very own umbrella-like cloudlet. I've drawn and painted this landscape many times over the years, attracted by its bare greens and browns and yellows, its simplicity and its round shapes. The ploughing teams of white oxen and most of the round haystacks may have gone but these are still my favourite Italian hills.

Monte Castello di Vibio

Ferrara

Ferrara is interesting, beautiful and not much visited – not at any rate by Britons. It stands in rich flat fruit-growing country between Bologna and Ravenna. There are a number of remarkable palaces, including the geometrically decorated Palazzo dei Diamanti and the Palazzo Schifanoia; visiting these gives one a pretext to walk along its pretty streets, some as straight as a Renaissance exercise in perspective, others medieval, tortuous and haphazard. Ferrara's galleries and museums are rich and quite unprovincial, clearly well financed and well supported: nothing seems starved of funds.

The visible life of Ferrara centres on the Duomo and the Piazza Cattedrale, an agreeable L-shaped space without any motor traffic. The Duomo's façade has a graphic Day of Judgement in which God appears taking the good people on to his lap like small children on to their mother's, while the bad ones are prodded into the mouth of a large whale-like devil. Other works of sculpture adorn the piazza, including polished pink marble lions by the Duomo doors; inside, in the museum, there are admirable reliefs of the Months, well observed and vivid. The most interesting present-day spectacle is the coming and going of Ferrara's many cyclists – passing freely through the piazza, carefree and elegant, their clothes and hair blown back by their movement, some bikes carrying two or three people; other cyclists stop there in twos and threes to talk, perched gracefully on their saddles. They make cycling look a sensible and indeed perfect way to get about – economical in space and resources.

Duomo

Castello Estense

The most commanding building in Ferrara is the warm brick Castello Estense, four-square and massive and impregnable-looking in its moat, its solid walls and corner towers decorated by only the slightest addition of stonework. The moat is now surrounded by traffic and parking space and market bookstalls. I made this drawing on a rainy June Sunday, from the sheltered terrace of a nearby café. This establishment, run by Venezuelans, was empty because of the bad weather. I enjoyed drawing the complicated perspectives freehand, and also free of any compulsion to get everything exactly *right*: a liberating experience if it doesn't go to one's head. Ferrara's perspectives, sometimes complex, sometimes simple and straightforward, clearly had a bearing on Giorgio de Chirico, a native of the city, in whose arcaded and shadowed surrealist townscapes the Castello occasionally figures. Antonioni, an artist as well as a film-maker, is another native; I saw in the town an exhibition of his ambivalent landscapes, vastly enlarged from tiny originals, in which – as in the films – the meaning has to be resolved by the spectator as well as the creator. It's not too easy.

99

Tomb of Galla Placidia

Sant' Apollinare in Classe

Sant' Apollinare Nuovo

San Vitale

Ravenna

Ravenna's one-time importance as the great port and link with the Eastern Empire would be hard to imagine or even credit now were it not for its great Byzantine churches. These are remarkable for the perfection of their solid brick structures, clear-headed and ingenious, and for their beautiful mosaics. This flat, deliberate and precise medium, formal and decorative as well as representational, is well suited to the shapes and rhythmic divisions of these Ravenna church interiors. The mosaic designs echo or grow from the architecture or, as in Sant' Apollinare in Classe, use a basic shape like the half-dome of the apse as a pretext for simple but beautiful repetition and pattern, almost childlike in their formal and careful arrangements of sheep, human figures and small trees.

In the procession of saints in Sant' Apollinare Nuovo, a mosaic frieze which extends the whole length of the nave, the figures are naturally flat and repetitive, their interest coming from minor individual variations in costume and gesture. The mosaicists must have grown very skilled by perfecting their technique during this early process of mass production. But where their skill, or vision, touches one most vividly and seems most inspired is in its minor details, as in the observation of apparently unimportant things like the way a pigeon stands as it drinks from a fountain. Noticing and setting an experience like this down so sharply and vividly is a poetic act. This detail occurs in the smallest of the Ravenna churches, the tiny Tomb of Galla Placidia. This modest building stands half buried in

the shadow of San Vitale, the most complicated of them all, and the only one in which the design of the building with its many complicated arches is as striking and as interesting as its mosaic decorations.

Standing a mile or so away from the town near the remains of a stout moated castle is the Tomb of Theodoric. This is an austere octagon, virtually undecorated, its bareness relieved only by the intricate interlocking shapes of its stones. Its flattened dome is oriented at a slight angle from the rest, suggesting a saltcellar whose cap has not been properly screwed on. Nearby are the rusty hulls and black and white or coloured funnels of the working port, a down-to-earth going concern by comparison with which Ravenna's past importance now seems remote and almost unimaginable.

Tomb of Theodoric

Bologna

Bologna stands in the middle of Italy's richest agricultural land and the crowded streets at its centre are wholly devoted to food: cheeses, hams, sausages, fruit and vegetables, big suspended fish that swing and brush against you as you enter its stuffed shops. Bologna is delightful, if surprisingly expensive. I spent a long midsummer evening in its great square, the Piazza Maggiore, watching the open-air life and activity of the city and the good use made of its amenities – the arches of the Palazzo del Podestà filled by café and restaurant tables, the Duomo steps offering a similarly convenient and central resting place for free, the young people arriving in the piazza on their bikes and motorbikes and holding court easily and elegantly on these unlikely-looking supports. The great Duomo encloses a vast and magnificently empty interior. The lower part of its singular façade is finished in coloured marble, but the upper part remains bare: it was left unfinished so that the money could be spent instead on building the city's famous university. It houses the lecture hall of the Medical School, whose flayed figures bear witness not to faith and superstition but to observation and inquiry.

At Bologna's centre are two adjoining squares surrounded by animated arcades. The Palazzo del Podestà has a fine medieval skyline, squat and solid: to one side of it, the Piazza del Nettuno has a spirited fountain [page 4] by Giovanni Bologna. A few minutes' walk away is the smaller and more irregular Piazza di Porta Ravignana from which rise two extremely tall brick towers, far from vertical but still even today suggesting the remarkable skill and resourcefulness of their medieval builders.

Piazza di Porta Ravegnana

Palazzo del Podesta

Duomo

Duomo San Rufino

Assisi

Assisi is a place of pilgrimage, an activity now symbolised not by Chaucerian bands of mounted travellers but by the vast sunny parking space at its gate. I hadn't been specially keen to revisit it, thinking that the tourism and the Franciscan devotion would be overwhelming; but even in mid-July the place seemed well able to cater for and absorb its many visitors, faithful and semi-detached alike. Everyone who visits Assisi is of course drawn first to the remarkable frescoes in the two-tiered Basilica of San Francesco. These are works of vigour, intensity and beauty. Here, as in Padua, Giotto tells his stories expressively and economically; the frescoes in the lower church are darker and, being by a number of different hands, more varied; the muted light makes them lustrous and mysterious.

Assisi is steep and the only level places are man-made. Pavements rise steeply in front of you, their patterns staring you in

the face; ramps make slopes steeper still; cars park as if defeated by the gradient; walking about it in the sun is a thirsty job.

The narrow streets of this hilly Umbrian town are clearly quite different from the Tuscan streets of, say, Siena – there is more stone, and the brick and stone alike are darker and rougher. The projecting eaves have shrunk back, so there is less shade. There are however the same delightful changes of level and of direction as in Tuscany, the same arches and half-hidden alleys, and the same dark shutters and heavy doors. The town extends between the great Basilica at one end and, at the other, the Duomo San Rufino, a pretty building in course of restoration standing by a sloping piazza, quiet and modest by comparison with the thronged naves and transepts of San Francesco. Above it, the castle of Rocca Maggiore stands high on a rock overlooking both city and countryside. On my first visit

while still a student, I painted the view of the surrounding landscape from up here.

At the centre of the town is one of those curious and inexhaustible Italian architectural surprises, the Corinthian columns of a classical temple (of Minerva) standing cool as cucumber between the austere medieval façades of the central Piazza del Comune – as out of key there as suddenly hearing a word spoken in a foreign language. Wondering why exactly the two idioms looked so very different, I realised that any classical colonnade is really a spatial affair, open and penetrable, whereas any medieval wall – however much it is pierced by openings – is essentially closed, a barrier *against* space. A gothic arch, even when it's supported by a column, is still an opening in a surface, a hole in a rock-face; but a classical column, even under its entablature and pediment, is something growing up into the sky, like the tree trunk it once imitated.

Via San Francesco

Temple of Minerva

Street near Duomo

Rocca Maggiore

Urbino and its hills

I've loved the pink brick-coloured city of Urbino ever since I first saw it forty years ago; perfect in scale, not too big, easily walked round, the whole place a happy mixture of splendour and charm. Urbino is surrounded by pretty hilly landscapes whose fields are steep enough to seem like flat patterns rising vertically before one's eyes. This simple patterned quality restored my self-confidence on that early student visit when I'd found the complexities of Italian landscape and architecture too much to get down on paper. Then as now these hills reminded me of the distant landscapes in Umbrian paintings, simple, muted in colour and rather toylike. Although Urbino has spread and developed since then, the hills remain rural and little changed, their strips of woodland and small round individual trees darkening as the summer advances, their patterns still those of agriculture rather than of developers and commerce. This, in Italy, is now unusual.

Urbino is dominated by the Palazzo Ducale of the Montefeltri [also overleaf] and in particular by the tall central portion that rises between its twin pointed towers. The Palazzo Ducale is entered up a shallow stairway round a courtyard. It gives a good impression of life in a self-sufficient and gracious court, tough but cultivated, with beautiful spacious rooms, some exquisite small ones covered with wooden inlaid pictures, and views out over the pretty hills. The whole of Urbino still seems under its sway. Its buildings are in part substantial, in part modest and jumbled, but unified by their overall soft colour. Its steep little streets are mostly narrow and, since cars have to be parked outside the walls, it's a good place to stroll about in. As in most Italian towns, there are good and inexpensive places to eat and pleasant cafés from which to watch the Italians which, as elsewhere, is one of the visitors' main pleasures. Urbino is a university town and the piazza near the central cafés is a meeting place for students, with their customary mixture of vitality and expectant hanging about waiting for the action.

Urbino exteriors are deceptive. I stayed in two hotels: one old and gloomy, the other new and expensive, a steel and concrete box so ingeniously erected within the old and apparently untouched brick shell that no one would ever have guessed it was there. The drawing overleaf was made from the hill opposite the Palazzo Ducale, from a viewpoint on a grassy slope, enjoyed by students revising, couples courting, and yet another pair of newly-weds being photographed in their wedding splendour.

Piола Santa Margherita

Overleaf: Urbino

Landscape near Tufo, Urbino

Piazza del Popolo, Todi

Todi and Perugia

Todi is one of the many pretty small Umbrian towns which stand on hilltops and can be seen from a distance silhouetted and pale in the summer haze. It is not striking or even particularly memorable, but offers the medieval Piazza del Popolo and a fine commanding viewpoint out over beautiful countryside. Even in hot mid-July it wasn't crowded but the piazza was pleasantly animated in the cool of the evening.

The Tiber, pretty but still quite small and unremarkable, flows round it; its valley to the north is rural and undeveloped, each hill crowned by a group of buildings or a small village like Monte Castello di Vibio. Here I saw a yellow caterpillar tractor at work on the kind of stubbled slopes that, near Urbino, teams of bullocks used to plough. But I also saw here one of the same tall haystacks, impaled on poles, that I'd supposed were now totally vanished.

Perugia is the Umbrian capital, an important, spreading city with a beautiful historic centre around the gothic cathedral. The ground drops steeply away behind its apse, as it does at Siena. The small streets here too are darkened and overhung by immense arches and buttresses in which the insignificant but practical human details – shops, windows, balconies with washing – are dwarfed by the massive masonry. Here as often in Italy there is a pleasant interplay between the same familiar materials, warm brick and light and dark stone. Perugia has erected a gleaming new post-modern office development near the railway station, brand new and flawless, but I preferred drawing the older buildings in the centre; they are less logical, less sensible, but much more interesting to look at. Here time, wear and tear, and the unforeseen have played a greater part, softening the stonework, making holes in the bronze lions and battering the gryphon's wings.

Perugia

Via Maesta delle Volte, Perugia

The landscape of the Marches

The Marchesan coastline is extremely Italian, an almost unbroken strip of sand and shingle backed by continuous lines of parasols and small beach restaurants, with every few miles a spreading village or a pleasant town. Back from the coast the ground rises gently but undramatically, forming a lovely rolling landscape of vines and olives and wheat, with occasional ridges of high ground, and dotted with hilltop towns and villages. It is fully but not destructively farmed, the fields of wheat and sunflowers still scattered with isolated trees or separated by strips of woodland. The drawing opposite was made from the edge of a village some twenty-five miles inland, looking towards the distant sea which can just be seen when it's clear. These landscapes are serene and characteristically Italian.

Tréia with its pretty skyline is one of the charming minor towns of the region; Cingoli is bigger and livelier, with a splendid weekly market just by its enclosing wall. It too is a hill town; at its top is a beautiful tree-lined piazza with the arcaded town hall at one end and the church at the other.

Tréia

Cingoli

Landscape near Cingoli

Rome

Rome is overwhelming, but seldom in the ways one expects. Many Roman buildings look oddly familiar to a Londoner's eyes. The various temples made me think of the British Museum portico, St Peter's reminded me a bit of St Paul's, the columns and statuary round the Canopus pool at Hadrian's Villa of garden centres and cinema commercials. Rome's most evocative things are the ruins of the Forum, and they are notable more for their historical and archaeological interest than for their beauty. But people have been impressed by Rome for many different reasons. The imperial British were fascinated by ancient Rome; what had happened to one empire might well happen to another. Now that it has, one can appraise the remains coolly and with detachment. And it is not hard to see why artists have been fascinated by Rome. In scale, drama, splendour, power to inspire, romance – the very word suggests the city – Rome is unsurpassed.

One is bound to react unpredictably to its great sights. It is exciting to see suddenly and for the first time things one has known about vaguely all one's life – the Tiber, the Capitoline hill, the Pantheon, the Vestal Virgins, the Colosseum, St Peter's. This last is certainly spectacular, with Bernini's famous colonnade reaching out like a lobster's pincers to embrace one and the funny little dome poking its head over the parapet beyond it. But to come unexpectedly on one of the great piazzas with their fountains and obelisks – Triton, Navona, Trevi, Popolo – takes one's breath away. Suddenly a narrow street opens out into a majestic space, surrounded by market stalls or café tables, while at its centre, spouting water, is a massive and theatrical piece of sculpture, like the great centrepiece of a table. To see and walk among such things is a great experience; to have created them, using space and imagination to give people a splendid place to take pleasure in, was noble work.

The most spectacular offering of all is the Spanish Steps. This celebrated landmark offers a variety of routes from the boat-shaped fountain up to the church of Trinità dei Monti, as the curving and swelling flights of steps part and come together again, and – just as important – provide a choice of level spaces where one can pause on and enjoy the views of Rome stretching away at one's feet. Whether seen empty in the early morning or crowded with midday sightseers, the Spanish Steps are unforgettable. Such experiences are not easily come by and they stick in the mind.

Rome has to be discovered bit by bit. It's easy to like the restaurants half hidden behind their discreet privet hedges, the pretty markets, the views down side streets, the columns, the left-over and unregarded temples, the piazzas and the great palaces, the Pincio Gardens and the Baths of Caracalla and the walks by the Tiber. But it took me longer to begin to distinguish between its various great architects, and to sense why the clever, adaptable Bernini was kept so busy and the unhappy Borromini was so astonishingly original. Bit by bit I began to get the feel of the various forums and the monster churches that pervade the city. I began to admire the curvy silhouettes of the baroque façades, flamboyant as merry-go-round canopies, all grandiosity and flair, and even to quite like the carved apostles swaying and teetering away on their dizzy skylines.

The Spanish Steps

Constantine and the Forum

The Roman Forum is the most startling and evocative concentration of architectural remnants, some fragmentary, some almost complete, with here and there a telling detail that by its perfection suggests the splendour of the vanished city. It's also a pleasant place to wander about in at any time, enjoying the temples and columns, and the distant glimpses of the Colosseum and the various towers and landmarks of the Roman skyline beyond. But in May it is especially delightful, bursting with fresh growth, with blackbirds in the trees, acanthus leaves springing up among the columns, and students and school-children roaming across the paved areas.

Before exploring the Forum it's good to get an overall impression [overleaf] of its general extent from the Via del Campidoglio on the hill at its western end. From here one sees the Forum stretching from the nearby arch of Septimius Severus to the Arch of Titus in the distance. As one looks, one can begin to see in the mind's eye not just the few enigmatic surviving structures but the orderly façades and courtyards, basilicas and perspectives of which they were once part.

On the right of this scene is the Palatine hill which in some lights still seems high, overgrown and mysterious. To the far left is the skyline of the Basilica of Maxentius and Constantine, its three immense brick vaults evoking Roman might at its most spectacular. Roman scale and command are evident too in the fragments of the gigantic statue of Constantine which used to stand in the Basilica; these are now in the Palazzo dei Conservatori on the Capitoline Hill. The clothed parts of this enormous figure were made of wood covered in bronze; only the bare fleshy parts, face, hands and feet, were of stone, and they are what now remain. The face is emphatically carved, as if to read well from a distance: from close at hand it looks strong and bold, almost caricatured. The nose, lips and eyes remind one that the powerful Romans were living people with personalities, not merely – as one sometimes feels – embodiments of power and will.

Palazzo dei Conservatori

Roman Forum

Roman Forum

Antoninus and Faustina

There is even greater intensity in the life-size portrait heads of the emperors in the Capitoline Museum – so full of character and conviction that one takes them unquestioningly to be sharp, vigorous living likenesses. Caracalla in particular has an alarming head, a certain implacable brutality – it's easy to imagine him as the builder of the enormous baths [page 134] that bear his name.

The most striking building in the Forum, and certainly the most curious façade, is the Temple of Antoninus and Faustina which stands above its lower western half. Antoninus erected it in memory of his wife Faustina; and, despite her scandalous life-style, he also elevated her to the status of goddess. The temple that bears both their names thus stands as a monument to conjugal affection and tolerance. In the eleventh century the ruined temple was absorbed into a medieval church and the fine colonnade was absorbed within a new Romanesque façade; but this façade, in itself a striking architectural statement, was later pushed back to allow the classical columns once again to reassert themselves. They now dominate their foreground of trees, marble pavements, fragmented splendour and pretty undergrowth.

Sometimes the things you see *from* the forum are almost as interesting as what it contains, and it has been too well tidied up to hold much romance; it has become an open-air museum, a superior classical theme park. But it does have great interest. The two triumphal arches are covered with wonderful sculpture; those temple columns that have been re-erected give a sense of the scale and the grandeur of the whole thing; the later church facades add their own variety of charm, and serve as a foil to the ancient architecture they derive from and imitated. The Forum is a lovely place to walk around, enjoying the space and the greenery and the absence of traffic. Part of the pleasure is in noticing and now and then sharing the reactions of other people – overwhelmed, awestruck, studious, curious, frivolous, bored, exhausted, fed up.

The things that have stuck most clearly in my mind are the fragments – a stone figure, a bit of cornice, a well-carved Corinthian capital left lying about among the leaves, not important enough to be carried off to a museum, but able none the less to suggest vividly how skilful – and how like us – the Romans must have been.

Roman matron

Giulio Claudio

Nero

Caracalla

Temple of Antoninus and Faustina

Pantheon

The Pantheon and the Piazza Navona

Most of the greatest Roman remains are treasured and securely fenced off or, like the Colosseum, stand somewhat apart, insulated by whirling traffic from the city's ordinary daily life. But the Roman monument I like best is surrounded by the most vital and rackety normality, amid the shops and hotels, restaurants and cafés, flower-sellers and beggars of Rome's liveliest and most eagerly visited quarter. The Pantheon is monumental and tremendous, splendid and unique. Yet it is also in essence very simple: just a great drum daringly supporting a shallow dome, with in front of it a vast portico of monolithic granite columns. The smallish Piazza della Rotonda in front of it has a central fountain surrounded by café tables. This is a good place from which to survey the Roman and tourist street life and savour the Pantheon itself, immense yet human, the city's best preserved and most enduring monument.

The Pantheon, like many classical buildings, owes its survival to having

become a Christian church. In about 1580, Bernini, who as an ambitious architect, put good and bad ideas into effect with equal eagerness and fluency, ill-advisedly gave the porch a pair of baroque belfries, fortunately now vanished.

Only a few minutes' walk away is another beautiful piazza, much bigger and more elongated, to which Bernini's genius makes a great and more positive contribution. The Piazza Navona is a perfect and magical space to stroll about in. The surrounding houses are tall and elegant. The fine baroque church of Sant'Agnese in Agone, by Bernini's more fastidious contemporary Borromini, is the central feature of one of the piazza's long sides. At its feet in the centre of the piazza stands Bernini's Fountain of the Four Rivers, a work of breathtaking skill and accomplishment [page 130] whose big arched base, strong enough to support a heavy obelisk, still appears light, watery and airy. At each corner is a figure representing a great river –

Danube, Nile, Ganges and Plate – each from a different continent. These gave Bernini and his assistants scope for more exotic contrasts and more interesting props than were afforded by their usual run-of-the-mill Apostles. At either end of the piazza there is a smaller but interesting fountain, of the Moor (again to Bernini's design) at the nearer end in the drawing, and of Neptune at the farther rounded end. The nearer end of the piazza is the more relaxed, preferred by the local people as a place to sit and talk, or to lie outstretched on the uncomfortable but handy iron railing round the fountain. The centre and the further end is almost completely taken over by fire-eaters, musicians, trick-cyclists and pavement portraitists, and by the black hawkers with their spread-out handbags, belts and trinkets and the armfuls of umbrellas that appear as if by magic at the first drop of rain. Crowded, bustling and touristy, the Piazza Navona is a wonderful and lively spectacle and intensely Roman.

Piazza Navona

Four Roman piazzas

Some Roman monuments were spectacular to begin with and still remain so, prominent and unmistakable, however much their newer surroundings may have grown up around them. The most obvious instances are the two great columns raised in memory of Trajan and [opposite] of Marcus Aurelius. Their purpose was to be noticed, to catch the eye, and only then, after that, to be read and understood, and the exploits they commemorate marvelled at. They still do all this admirably and – unlike the Vittoriano, whose PR function is roughly similar – without blotting out the view.

But a frequent and always delightful Roman surprise is coming across an ancient remnant, fragmentary or monumental, taking its place more or less unnoticed among the ordinary buildings of the modern city. Between the Pantheon and the Via del Corso, Rome's grandest street, is the Borsa or Stock Exchange. Its north side, on the Piazza di Pietra, is made up of a magnificent colonnade of eleven marble Corinthian columns, once part of a temple to Hadrian, built by the same Antoninus Pius who built the temple to Faustina in the Forum. The long thin piazza in front of it is pleasant but unremarkable: it's the colonnade that makes it memorable.

On the opposite southern side of the Borsa is the Piazza Sant'Ignazio, smaller and squarer but equally yellow, which is a triumph of ingenuity and artifice, creating an open-air stage-set to greet anyone emerging from the early baroque church of Sant'Ignazio. The three buildings that face it curve as if to emphasise the illusion of an amphitheatre; even the gaps between them have been as it were carved to form elliptical recesses from which further smaller streets lead off, just as the minor streets lead off the stage of the Teatro Olimpico in Vicenza. Standing on the steps of the church raises one just enough above the piazza to enhance the theatrical effect.

Another intriguing juxtaposition of dissimilar building styles occurs by the beautiful Piazza del Quirinale. The Quirinal Palace itself is where the Italian President officially resides: it too is bright yellow, but otherwise rather austere. The more flamboyantly baroque façade to its right is the Palazzo della Consulta or Constitutional Court, by Ferdinando Fuga; the obelisk nearby came from the Mausoleum to Augustus. This is a pleasant square, however important, usually with a sprinkling of sightseers and a generous presence of police; you can if you're lucky see the changing of the guard here.

Piazza di Pietra

Piazza del Quirinale

Piazza Sant'Ignazio

Piazza Colonna

piazza Farnese

The Campo dei Fiori and the Piazza Farnese

The Campo dei Fiori or Field of Flowers [opposite] is another delightful Roman piazza, one whose daily morning market makes up in interest for the square's architectural qualities, which are much less spectacular then the Piazza Navona's. At its centre is the statue of a monk, Giordano Bruno, burnt for heresy in 1600; it is thus both a monument to independence of thought and a reminder of the tyranny of religion. The houses round the Campo dei Fiori are tall and typical of the city, with their coloured walls, their brown shutters and their wrought-iron balconies. They have the extra Roman characteristic of grouping themselves together in shapeless and impenetrable huddles whose hidden extent and internal complexity the onlooker can only guess and marvel at. Here too are good restaurants and friendly cafés from which one can enjoy the spectacle of the market – fish and shellfish, flayed sheep, splendid displays of vegetables – without getting in the way. The customers vary: nuns and rich-looking townswomen, layabouts and prosperous businessmen.

The Piazza Farnese is a neat rectangle dominated by the great dark austere palace that occupies one long side. It was built for Cardinal Alessandro Farnese, who later became Pope Paul III; it was begun in 1515 to designs by Antonio de Sangallo but only completed in the last years of Paul III's reign by Michelangelo, who added the heavy cornice. I first saw it almost by accident during an evening stroll near the Campo dei Fiori, and was taken aback by its solid grandeur and immensity after the narrow streets that lead to it. It's now the French Embassy. Nearby is an only slightly later palace, the Palazzo Spada, whose courtyard and beautiful garden are open. Whereas the Palazzo Farnese is virtually undecorated, except by its own architectural forms, the mannerist Spada is covered in elegant, slightly lightweight figures and carved decorations: very pretty but, after the Farnese, a bit fussy. Its garden is a good place in which to pause and collect one's thoughts.

The chief roadway of the district is the slightly wavy Corso Vittorio Emanuele II, on which stands the church of Sant'Andrea della Valle by Carlo Rainaldi. The proper way to look at it is facing it, from its own piazza. But if you are walking or taking the bus past it, you see its façade from the side, well before you reach it, sticking up tall and paper-thin among its big black neighbours, a monument to the curious relation between illusion and reality.

Corso Vittorio

campo dei Fiori

Roman pavements and St Peter's

Traditional occupations and raw newcomers enliven the Roman pavements: film teams, beggars, people selling hot chestnuts or handbags, itinerant rice-engravers, the old flower-seller who each evening prepares her stock under the Pantheon portico, and the ever-present nuns and priests. The religious, in uniform or not, naturally gravitate sooner or later towards St Peter's.

You can catch a bus right to the back of Bernini's Vatican colonnade, but this cuts out a good part of the experience. It's more interesting to cross the river by the Ponte Sant'Angelo or the Ponte Vittorio Emanuele II and walk up the long straight Via della Conciliazione, built through an old quarter by the fascists in 1936. At the far end of it St Peter's rather pointed dome rises clear and strong, but the closer you get the more it shrinks. As you get nearer, Bernini's splendid elliptical colonnade reaches forwards pincer-like to receive and, if need be, shelter you; I was glad of it as an umbrella when it began to rain. It's all expert and theatrical and it serves as a sort of visual fanfare before one reaches St Peter's itself. The piazza is full of crowd barriers, as at a stadium or cattle market. It's wholly successful as a scheme, ingenious and perfectly done and highly dramatic: one can marvel at the geometry but find it all a bit overbearing. It is a forerunner of that equally impressive but irritating Parisian phenomenon, La Gloire. Inside, the basilica is overwhelmingly stupendous, with an exhilarating sense of many devoted people having come a long way to see it and having a good time. It's also big, confusing, and rich-looking, as if size and splendour had been its chief goals. But it is a pity that Michelangelo's preferred plan of a Greek cross was not pursued, for Carlo Maderno who added the façade and Bernini between them turned an idea with grandeur and clear-headed order into something of a backdrop.

128

Roman fountains and the genius of Bernini

Rome's many fountains may be modest or spectacular, trickles or cascades, but even the most obscure bring something poetic to a wall or a pavement; perhaps because they remind us of the basic human need they supply, perhaps just because of the soothing sound their water makes. The biggest ones provide a pretext for a great ornamental set-piece. The Trevi, the grandest and most famous of all, was meant to have been designed by Bernini, but his papal patron Urban VIII died before it could be begun and it was a century before Nicolo Salvi took up the task. Bernini's bravura attitude hangs over it all the same. In the Piazza Navona he had provided the liveliest and most inspired examples, above all in the great Fontana dei Fiumi with its vitality and flowing movement.

You can't walk about Rome for long without noticing the work of Bernini, both as a sculptor of genius and as an architect and all-purpose fixer of great resource and energy. His other works decorate or enhance, like the pretty ornamental angels which flank the bridge across the Tiber to the Castel Sant'Angelo – skilful and workmanlike figures providing a theatrical approach to the great castle, but essentially street furniture, conventional and run-of-the-mill. There are the striking and prominently positioned individual figures like the Trident fountain, and minor *jeux d'esprit* like the Fountains of the Bees, brilliant and lightweight, charming and a little jokey. All these are public, open-air works. For indoors, there are the two magnificent and moving groups in the Borghese Gallery, *The Rape of Proserpine* and *Apollo and Daphne*, youthful works of extraordinary beauty, vigour and poetry. Later came more rhetorical works like the monument to Alexander VII in St Peter's, clever and assured but too rhetorical and too theatrical for my taste. And besides the sculpture there are the monumental architectural achievements like the all-embracing curving colonnades outside

Fontana di Trevi

Fontana dei Fiumi

St Peter's. These offer an overwhelming and grandiose approach to the church façade, yet also inadvertently upstage it: after all these stupendous and brilliantly arranged columns, any interior would be something of an anti-climax.

Bernini set his stamp on Rome by being extraordinarily energetic, skilful and also by being in the right place when it mattered. He had a remarkable range of talents to offer, from the sculptor's mastery of the touching detail and vivid movement to the showman's ability to imagine and realise vast architectural visions like the St Peter's colonnades. Beside his work in restoring, improving or completing the work of earlier architects, as at Santa Maria Maggiore, he also designed his own very beautiful and unusual church of Sant' Andrea al Quirinale, barely 200 metres from Borromini's masterly Quattro Fontane. It doesn't matter if some of Bernini's work is over the top, or repetitive, or conventional and even almost automatic: it goes with the fecundity. Rome would be an infinitely duller place without him.

Ponte Sant'Angelo

Piazza del Popolo

Four Roman baroque churches

The baroque architects embraced the setting
as well as the building. In the Piazza del
Popolo, two churches, only roughly similar
but made to seem identical, divide three long
perspectives, creating drama and magic.
This is town planning on the grand scale –
the kind of effect that Wren hoped to achieve
after the Fire but wasn't allowed to. And
when in 1660 Santa Maria della Pace was
being given a spectacular new façade, Pietro
da Cortona extended the task to include the
flanking buildings and the pretty piazza in
front of it, creating a scene of great charm
in which the church, with its fine new
pediment, provided only the central feature.

By contrast, the busy crossroads setting of
Borromini's San Carlo alle Quattro Fontane
is unpromising: the streets are too narrow
for the dome to be seen and the interior is
cramped. Only Borromini could have
turned such restrictions into assets. The
remarkable façade, convex and concave by
turns, is laden with quirks: a shrine, a
diaphragm-like medallion, every second
balustrade pillar inverted to fit more tightly:
one can't look at it without sensing the work
of an intelligent and original mind.

Santa Maria della Pace

San Carlo alle Quattro Fontane

The Baths of Caracalla, the Palatine and the Pyramid

Immense and relentless, the Baths of Caracalla embody Roman determination and control – amazing in the height and symmetry of their ruins, but above all in the great length of the long south-western side that faces what is now the garden. It wasn't easy to find a good viewpoint from in front; the genuine ruins of the caldarium, the tall central feature, are partially obscured by artificial ones put there to conceal operatic lighting equipment, and trees screen the extremities; from behind, the tall ruins look awe-inspiring but a little dull, and give little sense of their great extent. I chose this oblique view in order to convey both the size and the complexity of this astonishing structure. It looks from the ruins of the nearer elliptical laconicum or hot room, along past the central caldarium – once domed – to the further laconicum. I drew it on a warm May day when everyone was enjoying the scene as much for its fresh and springlike leafiness and airiness as for its overwhelming historic overtones.

The baths are set in an area of wooded parkland within easy walking distance of the Colosseum and the Circus Maximus. This last long strip of grass offers good views of the Palatine, which from the Circus appears vast, mysterious and romantic, its high arched brick buttresses looking like a ruined railway viaduct. The Palatine looks best from a distance: when you are walking about on its ruins, it's altogether too orderly and well tended for any mystery or romance to survive, though its gardens are lovely and it has splendid views over the city. But from the Circus Maximus' beautiful expanse of grass below, towards evening, the Palatine ruins can once again look enigmatic, alluring and spectacular.

The most unexpected sight in Rome is the brilliantly white marble pyramid that stands by the Porta San Paolo, just outside the Protestant cemetery. The pyramid was a mausoleum complacently erected to his own memory by Gaius Cestius, but now looking a bit abashed and out of place in today's suburban setting of traffic lights and men washing windscreens. Its ancient Egyptian associations are irrelevant: it's really just one of the great simple geometric solids, as perfect as a mathematical model. As such, it is a splendid foil to the complicated and much tinkered-with Porta San Paolo just to its right. This is a picturesque muddle, forever amended and added to in order to make it more impregnable. The gateway, however interesting in itself, makes the pyramid look a monument to clear-headed simplicity and perfection: the slightest change would destroy it. But the whole scene is strange and surreal.

Baths of Caracalla

Palatine Hill

Pyramid of Gaius Cestius

Arco di Constantino

Porta del Popolo

Porta San Giovanni

Traforo Umberto I

Roman triumphalism

The arch, that useful device for spanning a large void using only small building blocks, was a Roman invention. It was natural that, having discovered it, they should use it not only for practical purposes but also for monumental and symbolic ones. Splendid triumphal arches, strong but beautiful, mark each end of the Roman Forum; a third, the Arch of Constantine, stands by the Colosseum. Rome, like Paris and London, had a stout defensive and containing wall, pierced by monumental arches. In London, little remains of the old points of entry beyond their names – Aldgate, Cripplegate, Bishopsgate, and so on. But in Rome, even now when the city has stretched far beyond its original boundaries, several gates remain as reminders of a frontier of the older city.

The Porta del Popolo built in the mid-sixteenth century stands where the Via Flaminia enters the city. Its exterior is rich in Medici iconography: glorification being its primary and naked purpose, it is proudly flamboyant. Its charm is in its interplay of white stone and brown brick, and in its pretty decorative skyline. The Porta San Giovanni is an altogether stouter-looking affair, in which the central stonework, heavily rusticated, is confined to the massive centre and flanked by bare undecorated brick. Both these gateways were built in the sixteenth century, and both took their place in the third-century Aurelian wall. Like the earlier Roman arches they provide minor pedestrian openings on each side of the main archway. In more recent times, most Italian archways have been put there to

mark the entrances to tunnels (in Rome, Genoa, Naples, and on every motorway) and they make no provision for pedestrians. The Traforo Umberto I shortens car journeys in Rome by tunnelling under the gardens of the Quirinal Palace.

While the purpose of the ornamental archways was to emphasise a stage on a journey, the point of the Vittoriano is to mark the journey's end and to call a halt, a full stop. You can sense this even from the Piazza del Popolo as soon as you see its massive white marble form blocking the view at the far end of the Corso. In some lights and from a safe distance the Vittoriano is very pretty. Looked at more closely it merely enshrines the Latin tastes for irrationality, reverence, conformity, and bombast. It's quite funny, but building it at all was a mistake.

The Vittoriano

Hadrian's Villa

Hadrian's Villa at Tivoli

Ruins should look enigmatic, imprecise and precarious. One should be able to marvel not only at their immense size or erstwhile magnificence, but at their having survived at all; they should look as though they might still fall on you, and they should also have dramatic silhouettes. Ideally these should be softened by self-seeded foliage, though now this is seldom allowed to establish itself, or even take root at all.

The most spectacular and most picturesque Roman ruins are those of Hadrian's Villa at Tivoli. They are immense and extensive; and after the urban settings of the Colosseum and the Forum, the villa's rural surroundings, twenty miles out of the city, are an additional pleasure. Here you can imagine more easily how the eighteenth-century visitors might have felt as they explored the heavily overgrown ruins and the grassy pastures of the Forum in what is now central Rome. The most obviously picturesque aspect of Hadrian's Villa is the long narrow Canopus pool, with its distant Temple of Serapis and its semicircular colonnades, the inspiration for so much plasterwork in so many garden centres. But I prefer the great overarching architectural ruins, and especially the magnificently vaulted and domed baths. These, like the ancient and dusty olive trees growing on their terraces, have kept some essential features of their structure more or less intact despite the erosions of time: one can replace in one's mind's eye the missing stones of the one and the gnarled and vanished limbs of the other, and imagine them both as they once were. You walk round them to the sounds of birds and the crowing of cocks; horses stand in a field nearby; the place feels rural and tranquil. But there's a snag. The only false notes at Hadrian's Villa are the information boards; each one carries prominently the commercial logo of an American tobacco company. Cultural sponsorship should not have been allowed to be so brazenly intrusive, so nakedly and offensively self-serving.

Only a short bus ride away from Hadrian's Villa is the town of Tivoli and the famous formal gardens of the Villa d'Este. They were much visited by musicians, writers and painters, when the gardens had become for a while overgrown ruins. They are magnificent and curious, decorative and inventive, but nowhere near as interesting as Hadrian's Villa. Such judgements are of course subjective; maybe I was just fed up or worn out by the time I got there. But it's Hadrian's Villa that I'd go back to.

Praetorium

Great Baths

Naples and the South

The Italian South is another country, wilder and poorer. Its one great city, Naples, is full of churches and castles, shortchangers and footpads; its houses are coloured in bright reds and yellows and greens; its hills are pierced by tunnels and funiculars, and topped by castles and monasteries. I like the Castel Nuovo with its frilly stone skirts, the Galleria, the Royal Palace, the muddled and beautiful old town, the docks with their aloof white cruise liners, and Vesuvius sweltering away in the haze. The city is full of the panoply of Bourbon despotism: castles, forts, statues of kings, baroque churches, and vivid images of death. Neapolitan *pensiones* are tucked away on upper floors, reached by ancient and unreliable-looking coin-fed lifts enclosed in wire netting. The whole place with its banana trees and cacti feels halfway to Africa.

Whatever Naples' history, it's the life of today that makes it most interesting. But the distant past is close at hand, in Pompeii and Paestum. Pompei evokes the ancient past more touchingly than Rome does, because it is so imbued with people's frailty and impermanence, which were not Roman preoccupations. Paestum's three Greek temples are set in a rural site by the sea, their stones full of the same perfection and the same irrepressible lizards as in ancient times. But after these places the southerly provinces seem forgotten and left behind, even third-world. This can be a virtue – the rock-hewn town of Matera is a beautiful and romantic place – but in less extraordinary settings the sense of abandonment can be intense. The once important port of Taranto is now just down-at-heel: densely packed flats festooned with washing and political banners overlooking a crowded fishing harbour, the whole lot blistering and steaming in the heat. I preferred the Adriatic ports of Bari and its smaller neighbour Trani, each with a fine Norman castle and cathedral standing almost in the sea, with many curvaceous churches dusted by feathery palms. There is plenty more of this rich-looking baroque in the poor South, where its opulence now seems insensitive and even crass: most notably at Lecce, whose façades and grand gates are top-heavy with over-restored ornament. At the other architectural extreme, though near enough on the map, is the region of the *trulli*, the most elemental building form imaginable – just a curving cone of stone with a single opening, curious and beautiful.

I didn't feel any personal sense of danger in Apulia and Basilicata as I did now and then in Naples and Sicily. But I did sense an overall regional air of impotence, of provinces outmanoeuvred and left behind in the national race to grow and get on. This depression permeates the half-built and abandoned buildings, the broken and rusting cranes, the new motorway bridges left stranded in the empty fields with no motorway even in sight. These are the current symbols of the Italian south. But I felt glad for the sake of the ancient gnarled olives, not yet grubbed up and replaced by younger ones; for the wheeling, mewing buzzards; and for the croaking frogs and grasshoppers and black snakes who for the time being have things pretty much their own way.

Via Tribunali, Naples

Port and Vesuvius

Naples

Naples is certainly romantic, with its palaces and fortresses and hills, its old crumbling left-overs, its businesslike docks and container port and the distant presence of Vesuvius beyond the long hazy curve of the bay. It's also alarming and sinister: a place where you have to keep your wits about you or get mugged. In its busy shopping streets you can feel safe and protected and comfortably surrounded by harmless people but then suddenly isolated and vulnerable if you stray a few steps off course. There is a newish Naples of extensive tunnels and fly-overs and a gleaming cluster of tall new buildings near the station, but the older city is prettier and odder.

Naples is built in an unusually rich mixture of styles. The newer city is the colour of concrete, white and sunlit against the sky and beside the almost tropical greenery and clumped palm-trees of its gardens and squares. Many of the grander eighteenth- and nineteenth-century buildings are coloured in the city's characteristic bright reds and deep yellows and greens. But the oldest monuments, like the Porta Capuana and the Castel Nuovo, are of strongly contrasting black and white stonework, severe and solid yet handsome and decorative. The Porto Capuana is a brutally strong fortified archway, once at the city's edge though now left high and dry as Naples has spread far beyond it; but still one of its great landmarks. The Castel Nuovo appears in many old prints and paintings, easily recognisable by the fluted and spiralling skirts of its stout corner towers. There is a beautiful carved bas-relief over the main entrance but the courtyard inside is uninteresting: there is more colour and interest in the pretty flower market down in the old moat beside the most curiously decorated of the towers.

One day as I was strolling aimlessly about in front of the railway station several men surrounded me feeling for my wallet, and I felt both outraged and very silly for letting it happen at all. After that I left anything I didn't need in the hotel, tried not to look vague, and stayed on the big streets after dusk. To get lost in Naples would not be a good idea: it would simply be very foolish.

Castel Nuovo

Neapolitan façade and structure

The main north–south thoroughfare in central Naples is the long straight Via Toledo which connects the Piazza del Plebiscito with the Archaeological Museum. Halfway up it stands the Piazza Dante, a handsome D-shaped space whose flourishing palms are backed by a curve of splendid if now slightly down-at-heel façades. It was built by Vanvitelli, the architect of Caserta [page 155]. It stands fairly grandly at the edge of Spacca Napoli, the oldest and most interesting part of the city, and a quarter I grew to love. Spacca Napoli is lively and beautiful, full of fine old buildings and churches. Its narrow streets are filled with hung-out washing which drips on you; there are baroque courtyards with complicated arched staircases off them; its own theatrically crumbling arcades shelter admirable fish shops and pretty fruit and vegetable stalls. In its narrow streets you have to squeeze against the wall to let a car past; others fill its courtyards; it you eat on the street you see airliners coming in to land and smell scooter fumes.

Apart from Vanvitelli's unifying curving façades, the appeal of the Piazza Dante's buildings is due wholly to their prettiness – their ornamental surface forms and architectural decoration, their colour, their statuary against the sky. Prettiness and ornament, however, are totally absent from the Castel dell'Ovo (Castle of the Egg), which is as different from it as any structure could be: solid, angular, severe, isolated and practical, a symbol of unrelenting might. It was built by the Normans and rebuilt by the Anjevins; its very austerity is in itself striking and beautiful. It makes even the Castel Nuovo look quite frivolous. It stands on a small island at Santa Lucia, the point on the coast where the port of Naples disappears and the bay starts curving north towards Mergellina. There is no beach – a long rocky breakwater intervenes – but there is a fine walk along this stretch of esplanade, with the sea and the fishermen and the distant tankers to one side and a long insulating strip of gardens, complete with banana clumps, to the other. These keep the noise and traffic of Naples out of earshot. Peacefulness is the last thing anyone comes to Naples for, but here it can be found.

Piazza Dante

Castel dell'Ovo

Piazza San Domenico

Spacca Napoli

Spacca Napoli

Spacca Napoli is the nickname of the oldest part of the city. It has several examples of an unusual architectural device, the *guglia*, which from a distance performs the eye-catching function of an obelisk but, lacking such a hard-to-come-by asset, is itself made up of highly decorative but synthetic baroque ornament. Two piazzas along the main southerly street, the Via Benedetto Croce, each contain a *guglia*. The one in the Piazza San Domenico Maggiore is surrounded by handsome painted façades and there is a good café at its base. I like *guglie* for their artless if pompous pointlessness: without the practical sheltering function of, say, a market cross, they are like marzipan spires set up for no other reason than simply to give thanks to God and to look grand, and they do.

Most of Spacca Napoli's many fine churches are set along the Via Benedetto Croce and the parallel Via dei Tribunali. San Gregorio Armeno stands halfway between them, off a steep and pretty little street. Its purpose, like the *guglia*'s, is to be decorative: it's dark and mysterious and magical and glints with gilt ornament, the two organs being particularly rich and golden. It's easy to feel its seductive sense of mystery and treasure. I made the drawing one Sunday morning as a sort of continuous or rolling Mass was in progress, with a haphazard congregation that came and went, sitting in for a while to be replaced after a bit by others. The tourists were kept as quiet and respectful as possible by two neat and bossy nuns in grey, who also read the lessons. Here and there among the

carved baroque decoration were half-naked figures which, making allowance for the changes of idiom over the years, were not unlike page-three girls. The overall decorative splendour and the skilful and assured craftsmanship made me think of Edwardian fairgrounds and mechanical organs. Here, prettiness, silliness, and faith seemed as one. But there are more macabre touches just along the street. San Severo nearby has two brilliant and remarkably overwrought sculptures symbolising Chastity and Despair, the latter a man enmeshed in a marble net, and in its crypt are two grisly pickled human bodies; and the stone bollards outside the church of Purgatorio ad Arco in the Via del Tribunali are topped by brass skulls, whose venerable blackness has been polished away by many devout hands.

San Gregorio Armeno

Gesù Nuovo and Santa Chiara

The extremely narrow streets of Spacca Napoli open out here and there into small piazzas; at the side of one stands the church of Gesù Nuovo, with a remarkably boldly patterned but unfinished façade, on which the pretty little baroque devices are almost lost in the great dark mass of the whole. The stone volutes and scrolls above the side windows are quite muted by the usually flamboyant standards of southern baroque, but they fulfil the purpose of all such scrolls: to disguise the change of level between the lower side aisles and the main nave. The dark diamond-patterned stonework echoes the same surface, but cut in brilliantly white stone, which covers the Palazzo dei Diamanti in Ferrara. In Naples the dark colour subdues the violent angular shapes. I saw its interior, as thronged as a theatre's, in the evening: I remember its ornate confessionals, those essential features of the Italian church, placed like kiosks along the nave, and the people standing about in groups, tidy and respectable, and talking to each other before going home.

The Gesù Nuovo is almost opposite the bigger church of Santa Chiara, which was much damaged by wartime bombing. Its most beautiful feature is the quiet cloister behind it, laid out by Vaccaro in the eighteenth century as a formal garden criss-crossed by shady pathways whose vines are supported by capodimonte faïence-covered pillars. The two kinds of foliage, the bluish-green faïence variety and the living vines and fruit trees around it, sit well together. After the traffic and the incessant noise and activity of the Naples streets, this square of greenery is cool and peaceful. It isn't even very much visited. I drew it watched only by one or two children; a priest or two walked to and fro.

Galleria Umberto I

Gesù Nuovo

Santa Chiara

Besides its grand piazzas – Plebiscito, Garibaldi, Bovio – Naples has two remarkable enclosed spaces. The Galleria Umberto I is a simpler, quieter and less animated version of the Milan Galleria: its shops are closed, its café tables almost empty; people stand about under its central dome as if there isn't much else to do. Even as a structure it's barer, lacking in angels and murals; but it has the same architectural grace and fascination as its northern counterpart. The Galleria Umberto I is still a good place to relax in and take in whatever is going on. But the contrasting conditions of these two great Gallerias, the northern one crowded, prosperous and self-confident, the southern one emptied, echoing and left behind, reflect poignantly the wider differences between north and south in the country at large.

The other curious Neapolitan space is the remarkable oval courtyard of the Palazzo Spinelli di Laurino, off the Via Tribunali.

You enter it through one immense archway like a proscenium; another faces you like a backdrop; and there is a monumental staircase of Piranesian complexity and magnificence by Sanfelice, who perfected this Neapolitan speciality. The surrounding palazzo seems quiet and forgotten, but by choice rather than necessity; the visitor feels tolerated here rather than welcomed. Spacca Napoli was having an open day and it wasn't hard to look around; but when I came back the day after, I had to make the drawing very quickly, under the caretaker's nervous and disapproving eye.

Naples is intriguing and occasionally alarming; it's also vital and often beautiful. I've been there twice recently and, having learnt to watch my step, have grown to like it. It has its extremes, its different cultures, its oddities; and it has its uncomfortable contrasts, between for example the pristine funnels of the cruise liners and the city's own picturesque but cut-throat poverty.

Palazzo Spinelli di Laurino

Pompeii

To visit Pompeii is an extraordinary
experience: a short suburban train ride out
to Naples on the Circumvesuvian railway, a
five-minutes' walk among humdrum villas
and cafés, and suddenly one is flung back
two millennia into the streets and houses
and baths and courtyards, the forum and
theatre and arena of the ancient city, all in
the still faintly menacing presence of the
looming volcano. The Roman Forum, too,
is evocative; but there what one senses is
vanished grandeur, glory and immensity,
rather than humanity. At Pompeii, one
senses instead the realities of ordinary
existence: one can walk along the same
wheel-rutted paved streets, not quite
straight or level despite the firm grid layout
of the city; flop down in the hot sun on the
same stone blocks that used to serve as
stepping stones across the muddy Pompeian
roadway, or by the same stone fountain with
its carved motif; see the election candidates'
names painted confidently and quickly on
the walls; and see the simple but ingenious
way in which corn was ground, between
conical mill-wheels once turned by capstan
but now standing idly like sculpture in a
grassy overgrown courtyard.

Pompeii has its great monuments too –
the Forum, the Basilica, the Temple of
Apollo, the Theatre; and its houses with
their inner courtyards, pavements,
fragments of decoration, bits of bronze
sculpture and hints of vanished wealth.
And there are the touching plaster casts of
the people overwhelmed by the falling ash,
their despairing bodies more pitiable than
the sculptured figures they half resemble.

Even in late October, Pompeii was hot
and crowded. But late in the afternoon
towards dusk, most of the people had
drifted off exhausted. I remember walking
back with my wife and son the whole length
of the Via dell'Abbondanza and seeing the
sun setting through an archway, with hardly
anyone else about except some guardians
eager to get home, and with Vesuvius a dark
silhouette against the evening sky.

Courtyard

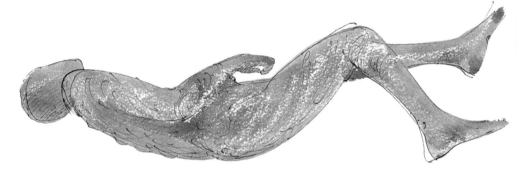

Pompeiian figure

Via di Mercurio

Bakery

150

overleaf: Amalfi

Forum

Capaccio

Capaccio

Monte Sant'Andrea

The Cilento hills

Capaccio

Amalfi, Cilento, Caserta, and Paestum

Naples and Pompeii are separated from Salerno and the south by the beautiful Sorrento peninsula. Amalfi [pages 152–153] is on its southern coast, its streets and alleys reaching up into the vineyards and the romantically craggy hills above it. It looks best from the harbour, where you can enjoy its fine situation without having to take in too much of the detail. Being still a very pretty town, not too far off the motorway, Amalfi is busy and full of visitors. In early autumn it was still warm and alluring, an example of that finely balanced Italian genre in which the charm just about outweighs the commerce. But it's a close-run thing: its surviving paper mill by a stream had given itself over to the tourist market quite shamelessly. The splendidly striped cathedral, the Duomo Sant'Andrea, stands at the top of a long flight of steps; behind it is a beautiful cloister. In Naples, the narrow streets seem drawn together by their strings of washing; but in Amalfi, the walls have to be held apart by stout arches. You have to choose between regretting that Amalfi isn't any longer what it was, and

enjoying it before it gets worse.

The Cilento hills rise behind Paestum. On their lower slopes are small and pretty villages like Capaccio with their delicately detailed churches and houses. Such villages often have beautiful old centres but are now surrounded by their own spreading and undistinguished suburbs. The higher slopes, where not too craggy, are wooded with sweet chestnuts. On the late October Sunday I was there, many people had driven into these hills to gather them and were loading up their cars and three-wheelers with sacks full of the same chestnuts that I saw roasting on the pavements of Rome a day or two later. Higher up still, the trees thin out and the hills begin to look like a moon landscape of bare limestone pavement, like parts of the West Riding.

Caserta is an enormous palace skilfully built by Vanvitelli (of the Piazza Dante) in the 1750s. Its triumphant central feature is the great staircase, ingenious, splendid and magnificent. But the rooms it leads to are immense, empty and dull – it's hard to imagine it ever having become the southern

Versailles it was meant to be, harder to work out at whose expense the attempt was made. Vanvitelli also designed the tremendous park behind it, with its long rising vista of basins and fountains and Vanvitelli's own lively sculptural group of Diana and Actaeon. There is also an ornamental area, with ponds and lawns, lush southern palms and exotic foliage, oddly named the English Garden.

On the narrow strip of flat land between the Cilento hills and the sea stands the ancient Greek settlement of Paestum. Three great Doric temples stand well separated from each other on its dead flat fields, roofless but well enough preserved for one to imagine each as a complete building. The immense Temple of Neptune [overleaf] is the most complicated, its Doric columns holding up a well preserved entablature and enclosing a delicate two-tiered inner chamber. The site includes a forum and an amphitheatre, but its chief pleasure is the chance it offers to wander around among the temples enjoying the sense of space and of the past, the open air and the stones against the dark hills.

Caserta

Paestum

Vieste

By the time they've reached Campania and Basilicata and Apulia, the Apennines have lost their sharpness and drama, but they still effectively divide Italy in two. On the eastern or Adriatic side, the older towns have rather a Greek air, with simple white blocks piled sunlit against the sky and steep streets crossed by tunnel-like arches which frame a glimpse of distant blue sea. Vieste, at the tip of the Gargano peninsula, is such a place, its old town a beautiful and complicated muddle of pretty houses clustering round a towered and domed church. There is an active fishing port with highly mechanised boats – the poor fish don't stand a chance. The centre of Vieste is extremely picturesque with its steep alleys, but its most striking feature is the rocky promontory where the houses and the tunnelled paths cling insecurely to the cliff. The sunlit limestone is brilliantly white and to the north of the town it forms tall white rockstacks on the beach and spectacular grottoes beneath the white cliffs.

Vieste

Trani

Trani is one of the string of historic southern Adriatic seaports; Bari and Brindisi are much bigger and more important but Trani has great charm. A wide quayside curves round a basin full of fishing craft and berths for yachts, backed by big arched buildings and barrack-like port offices: parts of these have been turned into bars and cafés in which tough-looking fishermen eat ice-cream.

There are several pretty churches, but Trani's most remarkable building is the tall cathedral of San Nicola Pellegrini that stands almost at the water's edge, angular and austere but with delicate carvings on its façade: they include some elephants. There is a lower church underneath. The effect of this great isolated building by the wide unbroken sea is like a vision of simplicity in which all the inessentials – apart from a streetlamp or two – have gone.

It's hard to say precisely what happy blend of setting and architecture gives a place charm. But Trani, with its net-mending and its quayside fish trolleys and its arcaded waterside restaurant run by a man with a white cockatoo, has this lucky mixture. I'd like to go back there.

San Nicola Pellegrini, Trani

Matera

The modern town of Matera, in a hilly inland region of Basilicata, though in itself unremarkable, stands on the edge of an extraordinary spectacle. The near side of the limestone gorge beneath it has been hollowed out to form the lower town whose innumerable dwellings and ancient churches have been hollowed out of the living rock. Whether seen in close-up from among the rock forms and the mysterious dark doorways, or from far away on the other side of the gorge, the lower town looks astonishing: the whole surface riddled with dwellings, some partially constructed, some entirely hollowed out. Most of the habitable houses have been condemned and shut up as being unsuitable for habitation; it's said that they were so often used by film makers – Pasolini and others – for their spectacular air of desolation that they were giving Southern Italy a notoriously bad name. Now the doors are mostly filled in with concrete breeze blocks, though some of the more accessible houses seem to have been reprieved and are being reoccupied and gentrified, with flowers in the windows and cars on the forecourts. The others are full of mattresses and old doors, bits of wrought iron and excrement: they must have looked a lot better in Pasolini's time.

The most beautiful interiors, because they have been the best looked after, are those of the churches. Some of these are dark and mysteriously subterranean, reached by descending several flights of steps, but unlike the ruined houses they are dry and clean and one's eyes quickly adapt to the gloom. Some of the small churches have remnants of interesting wall paintings and reflect a Byzantine influence. They are beautiful to draw because of the subtlety of their shapes, which instead of mechanical geometrical rigidity have a certain freedom and flow. There are no perfect arcs or true verticals: every line flows into the next, as if the places were works of sculpture rather than of architecture; they reminded me of Indian rock temples. From here the ruins hide the modern town with its offices and radio masts, and one can prowl at will about the rocks or draw undisturbed among the poppies and harebells.

I made the drawing opposite from the far end of the caves or *sassi*, to the sounds of hawks crying, the shrieks and beating wings of swifts, and the croaking of frogs down in the river Gravina at the bottom of the gorge. There are other more rudimentary caves beside the road that leads from Matera to the rocky heights opposite; here I tripped over a big black snake.

sassi

cave church

Matera

Six Apulian castles

The most perfect and yet most essentially decorative castle I know sits perched on an Apulian hilltop just like the Ark on Ararat. From the plain at its feet it looks splendidly isolated; its café and restaurant are scrupulously hidden among the surrounding pines. Castel del Monte was never meant to be military in purpose, but rather to embody the taste and sensibility of the Holy Roman Emperor Frederick II of Hohenstaufen. The eight tremendous octagonal towers that surround its small courtyard are simple and severe externally but exquisitely delicate in structure within; they repeat one another identically. The variations of the light falling on the flat surfaces as they turn away from the sun are tantalisingly subtle: from direct sunlight, through the sparkling midway surface on which the light merely glances, to the deeply shadowed parts where only reflected light can reach. The castle is surrounded by thrusting life – by deep grass and lush flowering weeds, with bees and butterflies and, as I noticed when I stopped drawing to stretch my legs, another black and no doubt harmless snake. I was glad to see this wild survivor undeterred by the concrete and the tarmac of the new road.

Other Apulian castles are less elegant and less aesthetic but more practical and more to the point. Gioia del Colle is a massive rectangular block rising harsh, impregnable and compact above the little houses of this minor southern town. Lucera by contrast is a far-flung affair whose many-bastioned wall encircles an extensive prairie. But Lucera is more interesting as an element in the landscape than as a structure, apart from one fine and complicated tower set above an angular corner bastion. This is the only instance I can remember of a castle wall enclosing a whole vast pastoral landscape. It too, like Castel del Monte, is on a hilltop, overlooking a distant landscape of harvest fields and brickworks.

Trani and Bari are extravagantly angular. Both are at or near the water's edge, with hardly a plain right-angle to be seen: nothing but points and sharp edges and sloping surfaces. But Taranto's comfortable round towers are in a wholly different tradition, fat and solid and ample. They are still occupied by the navy, which gives them a certain authority and an official naval air while the others have all become benign and toothless ancient monuments.

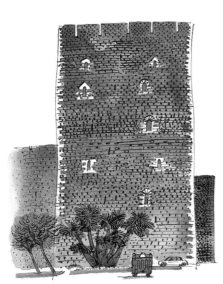

gioia del Colle

Lucera

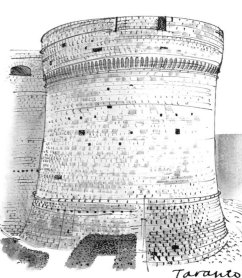

Taranto

Trani

Bari

castel del Monte

Apulian baroque façades

Lecce is famous for its ornate baroque architecture and especially for its uniquely inventive and flamboyant church façades; the interiors behind them are by comparison rather plain, as if all the real energy had gone into the visible exterior. But while they are breathtakingly richly detailed and abundant in their decoration, they are essentially two-dimensional; not solid shapes, whose essential forms come forward at you or shrink back, but flat cut-outs laden with pictorial material – saints, virgins, angels and putti, fruit and flowers, various symbolic bric-à-brac. They need to be read with the care and attention given to the small-ads pages: and the small print is no longer very interesting, having been restored with painstaking but deadening precision. Their great charm lies in their theatrical silhouettes, their extravagant volutes and broken pediments, arcs and segments, and their stone figures outlined

against the hot Apulian sky.

In contrast, Lecce's Piazza del Duomo is a lovely three-dimensional space in which one can walk *around* the fascinating and not over-restored buildings instead of having to gaze at them from in front as if they were pictures. This piazza is more secluded and withdrawn than most in Lecce, and more like a cathedral close. Not far along the street is the church of San Giovanni Battista, not so borne down by the weight of ornament as the famous Santa Croce – I enjoyed watching the Saturday-evening people coming out and standing chatting on the steps.

The most determinedly illustrative church façade of all is on the Madonna delle Grazie in Gravina di Puglia. A great spread eagle, the armorial symbol of Bishop Vincenzo Giustiniani, glares fiercely down on the platforms of a sleepy railway station, the mid-morning sun just catching its carefully

detailed carved plumage. I tend instinctively to react against such pictorial architecture, but there is something childishly conceited about this eagle that is quite disarming.

The baroque, being essentially theatrical, is well suited to the triumphal arch. The Porta Rusce in Lecce is a fine example of this genre, skilfully done, full-blooded and flamboyant. It is a good purpose for the architect to serve, giving people's ordinary coming and going a sense of significance and dramatic ceremony.

In Matera again, the Chiesa del Purgatorio is not only beautifully three-dimensional – an ample curve swelling outwards on to the pavement, as well as an elegantly rounded outline silhouette – but is also laden inside and out with vigorous skulls, skeletons and crossbones, in whatever medium is appropriate – stone for the exterior, wood for the doors. The craftsmen did their grisly job with gusto.

Gravina

Lecce

Lecce

Matera

Santeramo in Colle

Trulli, cacti and olives

Dry-stone walls and buildings always look good. Their simplicity and apparent crudity are endearing: they make one think one could have built them oneself. The *trulli* of Apulia are too subtle and complicated in shape for this, but with their conical roofs and simple doorways opening into a single chamber they do have a toy-like charm. The most spectacular are in Alberobello, but this one was isolated in a hot dry olive grove near Alessano, no longer inhabited and serving merely as a farmhand's shelter. It was good to see it surviving not as a tidied up and commercialised showpiece but simply as a bit of the Apulian countryside that no one paid any attention to.

I saw other simple stone buildings, apparently purposeless, near the very tip of Apulia, Italy's heel. The olive trees about here are older and more gnarled than is usual further north: their writhing shapes are more interesting than those of the younger trees, and the cacti in the dry red earth make the place feel southern and African.

Presicce

Sicily

Sicily is a southerly island, almost in Africa, once beautiful and romantic but now rather the worse for wear. It's a place of rocks and cacti and lizards, of prickly pears and lemon groves, of palms and papyrus and lush spring vegetation; a land of big half-deserted farmsteads, bare fields and rolling hills and a snow-capped volcano; of the Mafia, and tourists terrified even of their Sicilian guides. But the island wasn't in the end as alarming as I'd expected. I wasn't robbed, and once, when I'd carelessly left the car open for a couple of hours, it hadn't been touched. It's said that the Mafia protects tourists because they bring in the cash. I felt by turns enchanted, alarmed, intrigued and fed up.

The island has fine Greek and Roman theatres and – after Paestum – the best Greek temples in Italy, though Agrigento has been turned into an overcrowded theme-park. It also has in the cathedrals of Palermo, Monreale and Cefalu its own unique form of Saracenic architecture; and there is a splendid crop of baroque buildings, especially in and near Siracusa and Noto, daring and inventive but often quite crude – work that ingenious local craftsmen could learn to produce whenever an earthquake meant running up a replacement city double-quick. There is however a plethora of late-twentieth-century concrete. Sicily has shrunk: one can drive across it on new motorways without touching ground, on pilotis or spectacular viaducts or buried in tunnels. The traffic is piratical but no heavier than the M25.

The Sicilian landscapes I liked best were the mountains south of Cefalu and the high ground in the centre of the island, with its curious towns like Regalbuto, Agira and Leonforte. Towns I liked were Cefalù, Noto, Syracuse, and Erice, a small place in the far west, though in spring it was bleak and bitter: the siciliano must have been devised to keep the islanders from freezing. And I liked the town bands, the old bent waistcoated men creeping about like beetles beneath the dusty palms, the time-worn street decorations, and the painted donkey carts of Monreale. But I hated the plastic Sicilian puppets. The real ones had silver armour; shoddy plastic travesties now dangle from every postcard shop, dislodging the treasured originals from one's mind and substituting trash. And this is what not only tourism but present-day life in general is doing to the fabric of Sicily.

When visiting a country, it's often tempting to wonder what it would be like to live there, to be one of these people? Was it worth coming, or was it a waste of time? Has it changed one's outlook? Have the people, farmers, builders, soldiers, priests, business people, industrialists, recently or in the past, made the place more interesting or beautiful, or have they spoilt and damaged it? If they have, had they any choice? And if things have indeed been messed up, is it just temporarily or once and for all? Such questions come most pressingly to mind on an island, Sicily say, because one knows for sure that when one gets to the far side, that's all there is to see: there's nothing else, only sea. But Sicily's present damaged state is really only a vivid instance of what is happening, less spectacularly perhaps but just as inexorably, everywhere else – in Italy, in Europe, all over.

Duomo, Monreale

Monreale and Taormina

The cathedral of Monreale is magnificent inside and out. The nave is decorated with rich and wonderful mosaics. It would be worth making the journey just to see these wonderful works: the designs strong and confident against their golden backgrounds, the figures alive and moving, the clothes light and floating, the faces and gestures touching and full of emotion. The exterior and especially the apse [page 170] is covered in fascinating and intricate Sicilian-Arab patterns. At a glance these look simple and tempting to draw, but they are tantalisingly complicated, like a visual fugue. One can climb up to the terraces and observe the decorative designs in close-up, and see how their interlocking arcs mesh with each other. They must have been an interesting and taxing job to do. From up here above the apse one can look down the Conca d'Oro or Golden Conch towards the ships and derricks and container gear of Palermo shimmering down in the heat five miles away. The once beautiful Conca d'Oro has been suburbanised, a monopoly board now covered with houses; like Sicily itself, it is criss-crossed by raised motorways but even so its great wide bowl is still a striking natural feature.

At the other end of the cathedral is a small square, busy with balloon sellers, festive firemen and policemen, pony-cart rides for children, the town band and a procession headed by a religious statue. Monreale was en fête when I was there and its main streets were filled with lightly constructed ornamental wooden arches covered in light bulbs, which turned them into luminous tunnels. The crowds, surprisingly, seemed wholly Sicilian.

Monreale

Taormina

In Taormina, however, everyone is foreign: British, American, French, but mostly German. It is pretty but overwhelmingly touristy, and it's hard to imagine it as D.H. Lawrence once knew it – I couldn't find his house in the sea of new concrete. Lawrence wouldn't have stuck it for twenty-four hours today. But why shouldn't lots of people enjoy such a pretty and picturesque place, and add their own feel to it? That's what visitors do; it's hard to know exactly when 'some' become 'too many'. Besides the inevitable Max Mara and Benetton shops there are others selling bad sculptures and lots more armoured puppets, but there are also stalls of almonds and other Sicilian nuts, local wine, and fresh fish; and I stayed in a pleasantly old-fashioned and run-down hotel with a nice garden overlooking the distant sea. There are pretty public gardens too, with a wartime midget submarine looking out of place under the palms. The steep little town has many Gothic buildings of black and white stone tucked away between the cafés.

The Greek theatre, crowded or empty, is splendid: magnificently situated, with Mount Etna and the sea framed by the nearer craggy and wooded mountains. The ruined bits of the theatre – arches and fragments of tall brick bastions – have been made safe but still retain a certain romance; in the amphitheatre, grass still grows. For all Taormina's crowds and vulgarity, the people sitting around in this ancient place and absorbing in the experience seemed intelligent and sympathetic. Touristy or not, this is a good place to have seen.

Cefalù and the mountains near Castelbuono

The journey by road from Palermo to Cefalù is unprepossessing to begin with, with ugly refineries and chemical works on the shore, but after the Catania motorway branches off the coast road becomes quieter and more rural and is fringed by lush vegetation. Cefalù lies halfway along the northern coast of the island. It is spread out at the base of an enormous volcanic plug which dominates the town and, when climbed, affords good views down on to its warren of red-brown roofs. The town, like Palermo and Monreale, has a very fine Sicilian-Norman cathedral: from the pretty piazza in front of it, the twin-towered building is half-screened by feathery palm-trees.

The harbour is small and sandy; groups of fishermen sit on the quayside to play endless games of cards; a bride, in damp and sandy wedding dress, was being photographed on the beach. The windows in the rough stone houses look new and gleaming, and suggest holiday flatlets rather than merely careful upkeep; but the overall look of the waterfront, with its big arched open-air laundry and its houses perched solidly on the black rocks, is not much changed. In any case, change is normal anywhere except in a museum, and not something to regret automatically. In a climate of change, what matters is to retain some variety and individuality. In Cefalù, as so often in Italy, the place that best reflects the older and gradually vanishing way of life is the weekly market. Some of its stalls are elaborate motorised affairs, unfolding themselves instantly, hydraulically and without effort, to reveal displays of cheeses and meat and clothes. But other older stall-holders have nothing grander than a wooden box to spread out their tomatoes and carrots and lemons on, and they still look as natural and as much a part of the Sicilian countryside as the good-looking things they sell.

Inland from Cefalù are pretty hills, with sheep, olives and bits of woodland; and near Isnello are mountains looking high and enigmatic and mysterious when half-hidden in clouds. It's quite hard to walk off the road – the fields are fiercely wired off and dogs bark. The villages are generally a bit dull but there is an interesting hill town, Castelbuono, with steep streets, nice churches and houses, and a fine if smallish castle. The town is a good place to spend half a day, and far enough off the beaten track for too many visitors: this gives it a sense of reality, of ordinariness, which prosperous, important and much-visited Cefalù has inevitably lost.

Cefalù

Temple of Apollo

Teatro Greco

Latonia del Paradiso

Ortygia

Syracuse

Syracuse and Calascibetta

Of the various Sicilian cities I stayed in, Syracuse had the richest and most curious mixture of things to look at. Its outskirts are rambling, confusing and unsignposted, but they contain extraordinary remains, and the old city on the island of Ortygia is dense and fascinating. You can walk or drive round it enjoying the stone houses, the fine fortress and the white rocks rising from a calm blue sea; there are any number of rich baroque churches, one of which – the cathedral – incorporates in one of its nave walls the tall Doric columns of a Greek temple to Athena. This is the oddest contrast of heavyweight architectural styles I saw anywhere in Italy, the Doric orders having been not so much incorporated as simply engulfed – yet the severe columns look noble and striking, just round the corner from the frontal cliff-face [page 184] of fiddly baroque nonsense.

Greeks, Romans, Barbarians, Byzantines, Arabs, and Normans all had a go at Syracuse. The Greeks left behind another temple, of Apollo, whose columns still stand isolated in the centre of Ortygia, still as yet unincorporated in anything else. There is an enormous Greek theatre on the mainland: from it you can still just see the sea over a forest of new buildings. There is a pretty Roman theatre too, lower and smaller and completely circular and cut from the solid rock, and more luxuriantly overgrown than the austere white Greek one: it looks like a scaled-down version of the interior of the Colosseum, but nicer. Nearby are the immense Quarries of Paradise, a deep and romantic hole in the ground leading to a giant fissure in the cliff face. This grotto would be a gloomy place but for the hordes of schoolchildren and other visitors that enliven it.

Syracuse has a port and a fishing harbour and the railway ends there. I liked the waterside buildings – harbour offices, a large Moorish house now used as a restaurant, and the ordinary-looking dockside warehouses that nevertheless seem essentially Italian. Indeed I liked the whole town, with its yeasty mixture of styles and civilisations, its long narrow Piazza del Duomo and its little waterside Fountain of Arethusa with its papyrus plants and swans. Syracuse looks exotic, tolerant and benign; its elaborate wrought-iron and flower-laden balconies follow a particularly Sicilian form, bellying out extravagantly over the carved stone corbels. My hotel, as is customary in Sicily, had a name like Bella Vista or Vista del Mare but looked out only on to a newer and taller one, left half-built.

On the way to Syracuse I had stopped to draw the hill town of Calascibetta strung along its precipitous cliff-edge. It was May, midday and warm, the wheat was growing, there were flowers at the edge of the field; suddenly Sicily felt fresh and magical.

Calascibetta

Noto

Noto is an oddity, a new town built on a virgin site after the previous Noto Antica had been destroyed in the terrible earthquake of 1693. To ward off possible repetitions it was equipped with a profusion of churches; there are handsome secular buildings too, in the same rich and expansive baroque style. Throughout, the town made brilliant use of its steep hillside situation. The theatrical opportunities offered by this slope were seized on and artfully exploited: changes of level, flights of steps, ramps, terraces, dramatically inclined perspectives were all used to intensify the drama of what were already inventive and extraordinary buildings. These were further enriched by sculpture and other carved details which are vigorous and assured yet also have a certain peasant crudity. It seems odd that in this distant and isolated place such a level of skill and inventiveness could have arisen so spontaneously out of nothing. Probably there exist everywhere similar unsuspected reserves of creativity only waiting to be tapped. Noto, like Lecce, had a good supply of easily worked limestone which has turned a beautiful honey colour. It was built more than a century after Palladio died, but there are many echoes of Vicenza in this confidently and ebulliently designed town. Since I made these drawings, the dome of the cathedral has collapsed; but the exterior, and especially the façade above its tremendous flight of steps, was more interesting anyway.

While the most handsome buildings in Noto are nearly all churches, there is one remarkable street of palaces with many richly decorated balconies. The fantastic figures that support them must have been the inspiration for the snorting dragons and saucy goddesses of the nineteenth-century fairground showmen. At the top of this street, facing everyone who climbs up, is the church of Montevergine: a simple but brilliant arrangement of curves and projections which, while looking flat and plain from a distance, becomes dramatically three-dimensional when seen from close at hand. There's little decoration, but this daring shape seemed to hold the very essence of baroque magic.

Some miles further up in the hills is the small town of Palazzolo Acreide. I arrived in its Piazza del Popolo about 10.30 on a Sunday morning in May; there were only old men about in the square in front of the baroque church and the Palazzo Municipale, both providing good theatrical silhouettes. The black figures and their shadows stood out against sunlit paving stones; the women only appeared about midday.

Duomo, Noto

Municipio, Noto

Palazzolo Acreide

178

San Francesco, Noto

Palazzolo Acreide

The hills north of Noto

Palazzolo Acreide has several other
remarkably ornate baroque churches, with
unbelievably complex and almost perverse
groupings of twisted columns. Here again I
wondered what they had ever been needed
for, and how paid for, in this now remote
backwater. Above the town is a far older
remnant, a Greek theatre in a natural bowl
in the hillside, so small that the audience
would have heard everything. It was fresh
and cool and there was some shade; there
seemed some point in having built it.

Here and there in the Sicilian wheat and
barley fields and in its lemon and orange
groves, stand large and solidly built
farmsteads, surrounded by barns and stables
and outhouses: big efficient square or
angular shapes in a landscape of curves and
undulations. The one opposite is on the
high ground above Noto, near the old town
of Noto Antica, destroyed in the earthquake
of 1693. Around it is a beautiful flowing and

shimmering landscape of green wheat,
broken in places by dry-stone walls and
outcrops and ridges of rock, white against
the warm blue sky. But I saw many other
farm buildings looking poor and shabby,
abandoned and disintegrating, sometimes in
the fields, sometimes amid rocks and cacti.
No doubt farming people who have cars or
scooters don't want to go on living in such
primitive isolation. In the process, the
countryside is emptied of a bit of life and
the towns acquire a bit more.

It's hard to understand the relation
between this empty and fairly impoverished
landscape and the extravagance of such
architectural lollipops – how on earth did
the Bourbons pay for them, and why indeed
did they bother at all? This question kept
recurring in my mind in these tiny places
with their vastly expensive churches. I was
there out of season; even so these towns
seemed bereft of visiting strangers, and were

certainly not in the way of providing for
them. By comparison with, say, Taormina
this was refreshing.

The coast near Noto is a bit dull; just a
tiny fishing village with a car park, a few
small boats, and thickly piled up heaps of
seaweed covering the shingle. But the Noto
road runs through pretty orange and lemon
groves, fenced by dusty cacti, which give
one an exhilarating sense of having come
very far south: almost to the southernmost
tip of Sicily, and further south indeed than
much of Tunisia.

180

Noto Antica

Regalbuto and Agira

All the Sicilian motorways are new and well engineered. There are fine tunnels, dramatic bridges and viaducts and long sections raised on pilotis as a sort of continuous flyover. But the landscape looks much more interesting from off the motorway, when it's easier to stop and look at the lie of the land and at the obscure but interesting towns that are strung along the older routes. I particularly liked the old hilly road running eastwards from Enna and to the north of the motorway, that takes in interesting and shabby little hill towns like Calascibetta, Leonforte, Agira perched precariously on its conical hill, and Regalbuto. This last was one of the strangest and in a way most dispiriting places I came across – its

flamboyant baroque church tower damaged in the war and now looking more African than Italian amid the well-tended palms of the piazza, with a farmer riding a mule and a mid-afternoon population of penniless-looking old men with walking sticks and waistcoats, sitting about not pressed for time. It was interesting and beautiful but I wouldn't have liked to be stuck for long in Regalbuto with no means of escape. Apart from the normal profusion of cars, it looked much as it might have done at the end of the war. It seemed innocent, left-behind, guileless and without menace – a relief after the sinister mysteries of Palermo and Catania, places it is unwise to get lost in – as I once did – as it gets dark. Regalbuto is

surrounded by expansive and empty rolling upland landscapes with brown cattle and sheep, olives and prickly pears.

I loved the Sicilian landscapes with their grassy slopes and hummocks and little lakes and their bare ploughed fields, dry and dusty even in May, and the sudden dramatic appearance of the hill villages. Agira, like Calascibetta, is stuck high up, though clinging to a single pinnacle rather than perched on a long precipice. Leonforte no longer looks of much importance, yet it still has a grand central circus with four quadrants where two roads cross, a fine church with a good baroque façade, a palace, and a complicated arcaded fountain, the Granfonte, on its lower outskirts.

Regalbuto

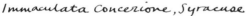
Immaculata Concezione, Syracuse.

Duomo, Syracuse

Four Sicilian church façades

The nave wall of the Duomo in Syracuse is largely composed of ancient Doric columns but the façade gives no hint of this half-buried treasure. Instead it offers a familiar mixture of saints and holy persons, skilfully assembled and disposed. One can stand back from these; but most of the Syracuse streets are narrow and its churches have to be looked up at. This lets one see the clever way in which the back-and-forth swing of the façades is organised. The Immaculate Conception is a lively and skilful example, though it's tucked shyly away in the corner of a tiny square. The Duomo in Enna by contrast is free-standing and makes itself felt simply and strongly, with an emphatic silhouette and bare, bald uprights. In their various ways, all these façades are about presentation: they make the fourteenth-century Chiesa Matrïce in Erice seem straightforward and guileless. Apart from its rose window, it's almost without external decoration, and its shapes are honest and structural. It stands aside from the street, on a bare paved area which isolates it and emphasises its austerity. It doesn't offer any flowing baroque curves but in its simplicity it is an admirable work.

Duomo, Enna

Chiesa Matrice, Erice

segesta

Segesta and Erice

Segesta is Sicily's most remote and most enchanting Greek temple site, hidden away among hills and artfully screened from its own car park. In late April the site was deep in yellow daisies and tall yellowish fennel which between them effectively covered up the flattened Coke and Fanta cans. The lizards scurrying in this fresh springtime growth were bright green, not brown as at Paestum. The rock was crumbling and the earth eroding from the tramping of too many feet, but the coachloads of visitors came and went quickly. The landscapes beyond the temple were wild and beautiful: mountains, hills, a plain, a limestone ravine. The temple was begun in 424 BC and left unfinished eight years later – there is for instance no fluting on its Doric columns – but it looks at a glance as complete as the Paestum temples. For all its severity, the Doric order is a perfect expression of order and subtlety, and the loneliness and relative peace-and-quiet of Segesta is an ideal and magical setting for it.

Erice is set high up on a mountain above the sea, near the western tip of Sicily. When I was there in the spring, the place was hidden in cloud; one caught only a few momentary glimpses of the sea down through the mist. It is hilly: its narrow alley-like streets climb and twist and plunge unpredictably, opening out here and there into pretty piazzas, and many of its houses are decorated with fine carved stonework. But its most intriguing feature is its intricately patterned paving. This is laid out throughout the town in lovely combinations of large stone slabs enclosing squares of smaller stones. The lines of this paving follow the curves of the alleys and where several alleys meet they create complicated stone intersections, like stone tramway junctions. The smooth stones tend to be slippery, so they have been scored; in between them grow grasses and small ferns. There is a pretty castle, the Castello di Venere, on an ivy-covered crag, but it is the pavements that would tempt me back here.

Selinunte and Agrigento

Agrigento [overleaf] is the most important temple site in Sicily but also the most disappointing: strung along a rocky ridge between a dull modern town and a dreary beach resort. The temples themselves are interesting and one of them, the Temple of Concord, is very well preserved, having been used as a Christian church. But the whole impression of the site is destroyed by rampageous tourism – the enormous coach park right in the middle, the traffic jams and the fumes, the metal barriers, the fast roads and flyovers and roundabouts in the valley below, the monotonous concrete flats filling the hillside above, all have killed its magic. It's sad, because the damage is all quite recent: until a decade or two ago this busy and commercial place must have seem quiet, rural, even poetic.

Selinunte, however, an hour's drive westwards, is still a beautiful and haunting place. The site on a flat coastal plain is vast and several of the immense Doric temples remain standing, backed by the sea a few hundred yards off. Most of them however have been tumbled by earthquakes, and their enormous columns lie dismembered and scattered among the dry weeds like children's bricks, or farmers' hay bales, or the big lumps of polystyrene foam that giants toss about in films. The site is well laid out and managed and is big enough to absorb its visitors easily without seeming overrun. The overall impression of space, remoteness, of ancient sunlit stones against the sky, is unforgettable.

Nearby but out of sight is the small beach resort of Marinella, just a tiny harbour and a modest beach, a line of bars and restaurants and shops and places to stay in, and a newly tarmacked road full of parked cars. This is what the last few years of the twentieth century have added to Selinunte – not too great perhaps, but harmless enough, and the best it's likely to get. Sicily isn't remote any longer: all one can hope for is that it will look after itself with care and imagination, and manage to take the long view of its own development. Maybe it will. There is still time for this to happen – but not much.

Temple G, Selinunte

Tempio dei Dioscuri, Agrigento

Index

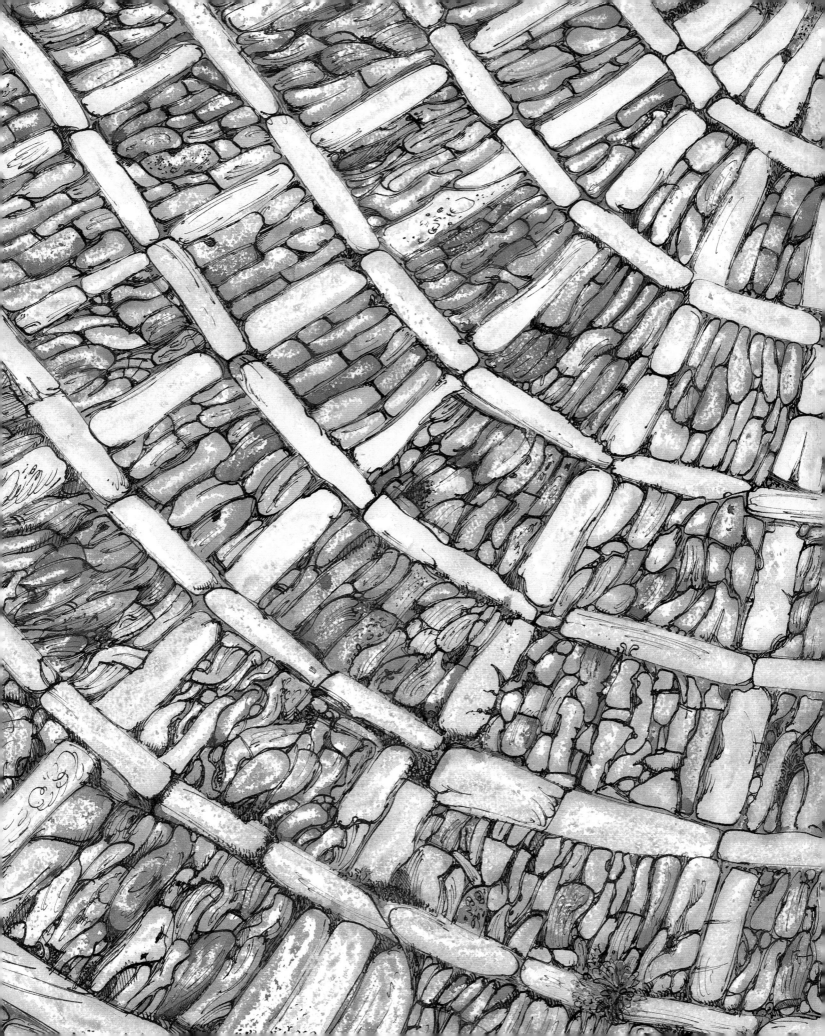